Comprehensive
KEYS™
TO
the Green

Comprehensive KEYS™
TO
the Green

Unlock Your PUTTING POTENTIAL
in the Game of Golf

ERIC ARMSTRONG

Book design by Jill Ronsley (suneditwrite.com)
Cover design by George Foster (fostercovers.com)
Project consultation by Holly Brady (hollybrady.com)
Cover-text consultation by Linda Jay
Proofreading by Alice Patrick

ISBN 978-0-9972400-0-9 (softcover)
ISBN 978-0-9972400-1-6 (ebook)

Published by TreeLight PenWorks
Mountain View, CA 94041
TreeLight.com

Printed and bound in the United States of America

To struggling golfers
who know that putting *should* be easy

Contents

Acknowledgements 11

Preface 13

The Story Behind This Book 17

How to Use This Book 21

The Big Picture 23

    The Importance of Putting 23

    The Importance of Feedback 25

Part I: Putting Technique 27

Putting Mechanics 29

    Set up and Stroke 29

    Direction Control 34

    Getting the Right Putter 35

    Distance Control 36

    Visualization Skills 38

The Putting Process 41

    1. Read the Green 42

    2. Find the Fall Line 43

    3. Judge the Break 47

    4. Pick a Target 48

    5. Prepare to Putt 55

    6. Keep Your Head Down and Make the Putt 60

    7. *Learn* from the Putt 62

Putting Philosophies 65

    "Power Putt" vs. "Die at the Hole" 65

    Uphill Putts Are Easiest 67

    How Much Does Excess Speed Hurt? 68

    Summary 69

Part II: Putt Feedback 71

The Science of Breaking Putts 73

   Understanding Vectors 74

   The Effect of Slope 76

   The Two-Dimensional Putting Plane 79

   The Effect of Green Speed 84

Learning from Your Putt 89

   Did You Have the Right Read? 90

   Exactly How Far Off Were You? 95

   Did You Have the Right Speed? 98

   The Finishing Quadrants 100

   More Speed or More Break? 102

Vertical and Diagonal Putts 107

   Straight Uphill and Downhill 107

   Uphill Diagonal 109

   Downhill "Slider" 112

   How Far Off Was Your Speed? 115

   How Far Off Was Your Read? 116

Fine Tuning 119

   You're Putting to a Large Target Area! 119

   Learn the Right Lesson (Practice Quiz) 121

   Maximum and Minimum Adjustments 123

   Making the *Right* Adjustment 124

   In Case of Doubt, Adjust Your Speed 125

   When the Ball Goes in the Cup 127

   The Ideal Entry Point 127

Summary: The Keys to Putting 131

   Green-Reading Principles 131

   Target-Selection Principles 132

   Speed Principles 132

   Putt-Evaluation Principles 133

   Self-Evaluation Principles 134

   The Importance of Feedback (Once Again) 135

Part III: Green Reading 137

Reading the Contours 139

    Single-Slope Curves 140

    Two-Slope Combinations 141

    Multi-Slope "S-Curves" 146

Getting a Break 151

    One Target to Rule Them All 151

    When to Choose a Faster Line 153

    When Break Doesn't Matter 155

    Optical Illusions: Putts that Break Uphill 156

    Walk Around the Hole—*Sometimes* 157

    Speed Saves 158

    Share Knowledge 159

    Bob for Breaks? 159

    Trust Your Read (not your "bob") 161

Part IV: Going Deeper 165

Special Situations 167

    Can't Find the Break 167

    Missed by a Mile 168

    Reading Your Chips 170

    The Effect of Grain 170

    False Greens 174

The Yips 177

    Psychology or Physical Skill? 177

    A Case of Forearm Tremors 178

    Fixing the Tremors 180

    Every Putt is a Straight Putt 181

The Mental Game 183

    Learning to Relax 183

    Breathing to Relax 184

    Confident Putting 185

    No Pressure 186

    Rating Your Putts 187

Part V: Bonus Material 189

Learning, Practicing, and Warming Up 191

    How Much Practice Do You Need? 191

    Home Putting Drills 193

    A Standard Sequence of Activities 193

    Practice Tips 196

Putting Practice 197

    Check Your Setup 197

    Short, Straight Putts 198

    Longer, "Lag" Putts 200

    Breaking Putts 201

    Goal-Oriented Putting Practice 202

    Two-Putt Game with a Partner 204

    Solo Three-Ball, Two-Putt Game 204

Playing Against the Bogey Man 207

    Keep Score More Easily 208

    Take the Pressure Off Your Game 208

    Make the Bogey Man a Moving Target 210

    When to Play for Par 211

Preventing Back Strain 213

Part VI: Epilog 215

The Pioneer of Vector Analysis 217

What's Next? 219

Glossary 225

Recommended Resources 227

    Websites 227

    Articles 227

    Apps and Devices 228

    Books on Putting 229

    Training Aids 231

    Instruction 232

About the Author 235

About TreeLight 237

Acknowledgements

It's unusual to thank your editor first, but I have to extend my undying thanks to **Jill Ronsley** for a superb job of editing that helped immensely to make this book what it is.

I'd also like to thank the many instructors who have labored so hard to develop a game worth talking about: **Ed Tischler**, **Roy Day**, **Bill Menkemeller**, **Laird Small**, **Bill Troyanoski**, **Gary Pearce**, **Pete Dooley**, and **Rich Bland**.

Thanks, guys.

I also want to thank my local GolfSmith (now Golf Galaxy) for letting me use their $5,000 launch monitor and accompanying software to practice my swing and dial in my club distances under controlled conditions. Their gracious policy deserved a mention!

I should also mention **H.A. Templeton**, who first had the idea of describing putts in terms of vectors, as mentioned in the Epilog.

I am grateful for the early-draft comments provided by **Jim Holmlund**, **Keith Shepperson**, and **"Shoreline Bill" Mykytka**. Those comments sent me back to the drawing board, big time, fellas. It's safe to say that the book would not be what is now, without you.

Thanks to **Mark Basil Plimley**, **Sam McMullen**, and **Karl Jensen** for their comments on later drafts, and particularly **Mike Pavese** for his detailed critique, which prompted significant improvements.

In addition, my deepest thanks to **Dr. Helen Shaw**, a great listener and friend, who came up with several brilliant ideas as I was searching for a title, as well as promotion suggestions.

Also, a grateful shout out to my long-suffering playing companions over the years, who helped me get started in this great game of ours.

Many others have helped enormously, often without even realizing it, so I would also like to express my gratitude to:

- **Yoon Cho**, for her support during the process.

- **Tim McCollum** for the title of the book he always threatened to write—*From Birdie to Bogey in Three Easy Putts*. With his permission, I stole that line and used a modified version of it for a section title. Thanks, Tim.

- Billiards team captain **Mike Chung** and golfing partners **Jim Holmlund** and **Scott Gil**, who kept asking how the book was going. Thanks for taking an interest!

- All of my other playing partners, who were willing to listen to my progress reports, even when they never asked.

Thanks to you all. I owe you each a cup of coffee—and a round of golf.

Preface

If you're reading this, likely you're a novice or average golfer who wants to improve. I get that. But like me, you don't have a whole lot of time on your hands!

The really frustrating thing was that when I managed to get near the green in a decent number of strokes, I was *still* shooting high scores. You probably understand.

I remember the day I was 30 yards from the hole in 2 shots, on a par 5. Awesome! From there, it took 3 short-game shots to get *on* the green, still far from the hole. Then I stubbed the first putt, leaving 2 more putts before I finished. Let's see: near the green in 2, 3 to get on, and 3 to get down. An 8. Eight! A triple bogey on a hole that should have been a par, or possibly even a birdie. But the short game shots and putts are the easiest strokes in golf!

Given any kind of reasonable swing, the ability to "go low" is *all* about the short game and putting. When you're anywhere near the green, you have to get *on* the green. In one stroke. *Reliably*, using your wedges. Once you're on, you need to be able to get down in 2, at most. *Regularly*, with your putter. There will be the occasional 3-putt, of course. But there should be more than enough 1-putts and chip-ins to balance them out.

Needless to say, I was frustrated. That frustration put me on the lookout for solutions. The short game solution will have to wait for another book, but the putting solution boils down to *correct feedback*—the ability to evaluate putt results accurately. (Which, it turns out, very few know how to do.)

Good putting starts with understanding how to read the green, of course. And I cover that topic in depth. But it is even *more* critical to know how to evaluate the results of every putt you observe.

That capability is the foundation not only for good putting, but also for good chipping and pitching. Because success in each of those areas depends on delivering the ball to a *target*. Picking the *right* target depends on knowing how the greens are working, that day. *Playing* to that target, meanwhile, depends on knowing how much force to apply to the ball. In each case, you need to *understand* how the speed of the green affects the shot—and know for certain whether you need to adjust your *read* when preparing to putt, or your *speed* when making the putt and, in each case, how much of an adjustment you need to make.

In the end, then, even more important than a general ability to "read a green" is the ability to derive the correct *feedback* from your shots on and around the green. That information makes all the difference in your ability to score.

It is that unique perspective on putting that this book provides. Because most of the effort comes down to *understanding* the greens, my approach ensures that you *will* lower your scores, in time, depending on how much you play or practice.

Now, I am not a great golfer. I can say with total confidence that there is not one single professional golfer who is losing any sleep tonight because of me. (But I'm getting better so *watch out*, you guys.) What I *am* is an accomplished athlete, coach, instructor, and writer. What I do well is to analyze problems, arrive at original and useful ways of understanding them, and then explain the solutions clearly.

With the insights I've had, my game has improved, certainly. More importantly, the frustration in that area of the game is gone! Now, when things go wrong, *I know what happened*, and I know how to improve.

In addition, I am 100% confident that my mind-body computer is busy crunching the numbers behind the scenes, and preparing to make automatic corrections. When it comes to enjoying the game— *and* to doing well—that perspective makes a world of difference. It's a perspective I want to share with you.

Comprehensive Keys to the Green combines valuable observations and explanations on *putt feedback* that have never before been published. It also contains a wealth of information on putting technique, to help you take advantage of that knowledge. Its unique perspectives and clear explanations combine to create a comprehensive manual that will have you *mastering the greens* in no time.

Putting is not rocket science, or brain surgery. It's not even "rocket surgery". It doesn't require extraordinary physical talents. It all starts with knowing *what* to do. *Comprehensive Keys to the Green* gives you that information, and provides you with a huge opportunity to *minimize your misses* and *dramatically increase the number of putts you make.*

After reading this book, I can't promise that you will improve your putting overnight. I *can* promise that you will significantly improve your *understanding* of every putt you make and every putt you see—and that, as a result, your putting *will* improve over time, inevitably and inexorably—and that it will happen more rapidly than you might expect.

In other words, I am certain that you will acquire deep insight into the putting process. Once you know those things, you'll be able to apply them to the short game, as well as putting. And you'll be able to use them for life, even if you don't play all that much.

In your hands you hold the keys that will unlock your putting potential. Grab them now, and learn from every putt!

Eric Armstrong
Mountain View, California

The Story
Behind This Book

Like every golfer on the planet, I was *motivated* to improve my short game. The question was how to do it.

I read books and magazine articles. I found videos on the web. I listened to the advice commentators gave during tournaments (which I continue to appreciate, and is for me one of the best reasons for watching). I found a lot of things that helped, but I didn't find any real solutions. Nothing gave me the *keys* I needed to unlock the mystery of the greens and put low scores in my future.

Then one day I made an important discovery: Even the best putters in the world require consistent feedback. They *need* that feedback to even be *good*, never mind great. The insight came while watching a televised golf tournament. And it wasn't the typically great play of the pros that awakened that understanding. On that day, it was just the opposite.

Even the best putters in the world require consistent feedback.

On this particular day, there had been rain that held up play for an hour or two. Patches of cloud floated slowly across the sky, creating moving areas of shade on the ground. Some of the greens were shaded by trees, some were partially exposed, and others were fully exposed.

Depending on the location of the trees, some of the greens were in permanent shade, while others were shaded only part of the day. Other greens, meanwhile were mostly in sun, except when a cloud drifted across. The trees also sheltered some of the greens from the strong wind that was still blowing, while others were fully or partially exposed.

Because of the variations in conditions, the greens dried out at different rates during the day—and none were the same speed as they had been on the previous day. Worse, as the clouds moved, the pros could find themselves on a shady green that had mostly been in sun, so it ran faster than expected. Or they might be on a sunny green that had been in shade. Or the sunny green might actually have been in the sun for a while.

As a result of the variations, some of the greens were fast, while others were slow. The shifting shade, meanwhile, made it extremely difficult to predict which was which.

Guess what happened?

Those professionals—those incredibly talented, practiced-to-perfection pros—putted no better than you or I would. I never in my life saw touring pros make so many 3-putts, and even 4-putts. They must have set a PGA tour record for 3-putts that day.

That told me something.

It told me that what we take as incredible green-reading ability on the pro tour is really a matter of having the ability to *adjust*—to learn from previous holes and apply that knowledge to subsequent holes. That's a major reason that the putting is so good on tour. Absent that feedback, they were no better than you, or I, or anyone else!

Now, clearly, it is important to be able to read the green. It's a necessary skill, in fact. It's what lets you choose the right line. But equally clearly, that ability is not everything. These were the most skilled green-readers in the world. And they couldn't make a 2-putt. But on a normal day, when the greens are consistent, they 2-putt virtually all of the time.

It was obvious that good results depend on the ability to take the right feedback from each putt, but what feedback could they be getting?

Well, there are only two things that determine whether a putt is successful: the line and the speed. Get both right and you sink the putt. But if the putt doesn't drop, *you need to know which one was off*, and by how much. The question is, how to tell?

Finding the answer to that question was the impetus for this book. It was, in fact, a *revelation*. Afterward, it felt like there was no green on the planet I couldn't 2-putt. That was huge. I certainly never felt that way before! By the time you get done with Part II, I suspect the same will be true for you.

I also investigated how to get *on* the green, but those answers have to wait for the second volume in this series. That one covers the chipping and pitching skills you need to get on the green, and how to control distance. But the same green-reading ability that gets you close to the hole on a long-distance putt also helps you get close on a short chip from off the green, so you'll find that this volume and that one work well together.

Hopefully, I've whetted your appetite for the next book. But right now, let's get back to where everything starts—the ability to understand the greens.

In *Comprehensive Keys to the Green*, I give you the keys to unlock that mystery. I also cover the mechanics of putting technique, plus a lot of additional material on green reading, tips on warm-up and practice routines, recommended resources, and a useful little piece on preventing back strain.

I hope you find that reading this book is as beneficial for you as writing it has been for me!

How to Use
This Book

USE THIS OVERVIEW to choose the best place to start.

Part I: Putting Technique covers putting technique and basic green-reading skills. After a discussion of putting mechanics, The Putting Process gives you a step-by-step method for approaching a putt, and introduces vocabulary that will be helpful later on.

The Putting Philosophies chapter at the end of that section explains why the "die at the hole" approach is generally more useful, and the times when the "power putt" approach makes more sense.

Part II: Putt Feedback shows you how to derive accurate feedback from a putt. This section contains the unique, new information that is the major focus of this book. And as the saying goes, "Drive for show, putt for dough". In other words, this part of the book gives you the keys to the *green*.

Part III: Green Reading shows how to anticipate the ball's movement as it encounters different slopes.

Part IV: Going Deeper dives into special situations like grain and the "yips", and covers the mental game.

Part V: Bonus Material rounds out the book with tips on practicing, an explanation of why most of us should track our scores relative to bogey (not par), and tips to save your back.

Part VI: Epilog takes stock of where we are when it comes to teaching and learning golf, along with my thoughts on where we *could* be.

It also provides links to the products and manuals referenced in the text.

In the next section, "The Big Picture". I'll explain why putting—and feedback—are so important.

The Big Picture

Comprehensive *Keys to the Green* offers you two main skills: how to read a green; and, arguably more important, how to evaluate a putt.

With these new skills, you save strokes when you're on the green, and those same skills will help you save strokes when you're *around* the green, as well. You'll get "up and down" a lot more often and give yourself the best possible chance for an "amateur up and down"—first getting *on* (in decent position on the green), then *up* (close to the hole), and then *down* (in the hole)—virtually every time.

Think about it: If you knew that every time you got anywhere near the green, you would take 3 more shots at *most*, you'd be pretty happy, wouldn't you? It makes the game a lot more fun, that's for sure.

In this book, we're going to use *vectors* to make sense of putting, but before we do, I want to take a bit of time to see where putting fits in your overall game. (Don't worry about the vectors. The explanations are easy to grasp, with lots of diagrams to give you a clear picture of what's happening.)

The Importance of Putting

How important is putting, really? Where exactly does it fit into your game?

Well, if you score par, putts are supposed to be 50% of your score. If you get on the green "in regulation", that leaves you 2 putts on every hole, or 36 putts for a round of 72. If you're playing well, putting is pretty important!

But putting is important even if you're not playing well. Short game expert Dave Pelz points out that putting makes up 43% of the game for anyone taking up to 100 shots a round. If you're scoring more than that, swing lessons are definitely in order. After all, first you've got to *get* to the green! But even for those in the 80–100 stroke range, putts are nearly 50% of the game.

While putting is important for the average golfer, it's even more important for elite golfers. Excellent putting is the hallmark of the greatest players of the game. It makes sense. All of the highest-ranking players pull off superb shots from tee to green. They have some duds (typically followed by outstanding recovery shots), but in general they are all playing well. The difference between them frequently comes down to making medium-to-long putts.

Every great champion won their tournaments by sinking long, "magical" putts at critical moments. If you wanted a poster boy of putting, you could nominate Tiger Woods or Jack Nicklaus—each was the greatest long-distance pressure putter of his era. Then there is Tom Watson, whose skill on and around the green was legendary. For a more recent example, think Jordan Spieth. He won two majors and the $10m FedEx Cup in 2015. In the process, he had the highest percentage on tour for putts over 10 feet—in addition to other statistics he dominated—one of which was *not* being long off the tee.

All of the skills from tee to green are important, and everyone on tour has them. They're a requirement. But skills *around* the green—and especially putting—are a key differentiator. It is the ability to sink long putts that is the difference between the champion and everyone else in the field. The better they can read a green—and the better they can factor in the results of previous putts—the bigger the paycheck.

Of course, back here in the amateur ranks, we don't get on the green from long distance with any stunning regularity. But *sometimes* we do. And *when* we do, we *also* need to putt well, to make the great approach shot count. If we take a 3-putt from long distance when everyone else makes 2 from closer in, everyone scores the same.

So, yeah. Putting is pretty important.

The Importance of Feedback

As I mentioned in the "Story Behind This Book", top pros playing in unpredictable, inconsistent conditions were putting pretty horribly—just like most of us! The key, given consistent conditions, is knowing *how* to take reliable feedback from the green, so you can *adjust*.

The adjustment could be in the choice of line or the speed of the putt, or maybe a little of each, or maybe a lot of one and just a little of the other. The point is: The only way to know what adjustments to make is to know how to evaluate the results of your putt. In other words, the putting process starts by reading the green, and it ends by evaluating your putt.

> **The putting process starts
> by reading the green.
> It ends by evaluating your putt.**

It makes sense that the pros were struggling. A slow green breaks a little. A fast green with the same slope breaks a lot. The amount of break you need to allow for depends on the speed of the green. But you can't *see* the speed of the green. You can only see the slope. And you can't see it by watching other putts, because you don't know how much force was applied.

To gauge green speed, you have to factor in the results from your last few putts. With that information, your mental computer can relate the amount of force you provided with the distance the ball traveled.

Without that information, you don't know how much break to allow. So your first putt is liable to be wildly inaccurate, and it won't be until after your second or third putt that you'll begin to have a really good sense of the green's speed. But by then, you're so close to the cup that it doesn't matter much!

The first takeaway is that consistency between greens is *critical* to your chances of a low score. If the greens aren't consistent from hole to hole, you don't really have a chance. So if you want low scores, the very first requirement is that you are playing on a course that gives you consistent greens. They can be fast, or they can be slow, but they must be *consistent*.

But even when the greens are consistent, you still need to make adjustments, and to do that you need to know what *kind* of adjustment to make. In particular, you need to be able to assess your putt:

1. Did it have enough *break*? Was it high? Low?
   If it wasn't on the right line, how far off was it?

2. Did it have the right *speed*? How far off was it?

The answers are important, because if you think you need to strike it harder when what you really need is to adjust the line, you're likely to see the ball go racing by the hole on a narrow miss—much farther than it would otherwise have gone. Or maybe, like most amateurs, you don't really know *what* to adjust. You need answers.

This book shows you how to get those answers.

Part I

Putting Technique

THIS SECTION OF THE BOOK focuses on the process you use to set up your shot, and stroke it.

If you're a beginner, or have any doubts about your ability to deliver the ball down your intended line, for your chosen distance, you'll want to give this section a close read.

If you're in firm command of your stroke, and you want to focus on reading greens and understanding putts, you can skip to Part II: Putt Feedback, which presents the unique new material that is the book's major focus. But even then, it makes sense to come back to this section, because it *never* hurts to master the basics!

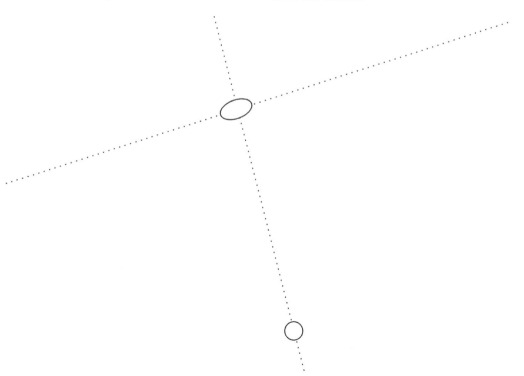

Putting Mechanics

Good putting mechanics are vital. This book will tell you what you need to know, so you know *what* to do, but that information will have little value if you can't perform the stroke. In this chapter, I'll show how your putting mechanics relate to consistency, direction control, and distance control, to show why they're so valuable.

I'd also like to emphasize the value of getting lessons! A book can tell you how to do things right, but it takes another set of eyes to tell you what you're doing wrong, and to suggest the specific improvements you need! (For more on that, see the sidebar, "The Value of Lessons".)

Set up and Stroke

Good putting technique starts with decent mechanics. Those mechanics will help you to putt the ball down the line you intend, and they will eventually help you develop distance control. If you can't putt a ball down the intended line and close to the intended distance, then green reading ability will be nice, but you won't be able to *use* it to lower your scores.

Putting Styles

In the next section, I'm going to describe the mechanics of the two-handed putting technique—the positions and movements that ensure a consistent and reliable putting stroke, using that technique.

However, it is worth noting that there are other styles of putting!

The Value of Lessons

I discovered the importance of good lessons early on when I was playing intercollegiate volleyball in graduate school. I had some early success, and was making friends, so I did some learning "on my own". After a year, I had gotten good enough to join some of my friends at a four-day volleyball camp.

To say that it was a learning experience would be to put it mildly. For one thing, I learned the necessity of being physically prepared. (I was so sore, I could barely *walk*.)

But the really big lesson was that *everything* I had been doing was non-optimal. In many cases, my methods were just outright wrong. As a result, even though the camp taught me the right things to do, I couldn't *perform* the skills, especially in the heat of the moment. The sore muscles and old habits kept interfering. It took a *year* to unlearn the old habits, so the new techniques were reliable in a game situation.

So the big takeaway was the importance of learning the *right* way to do things early on. That way, even if you're not doing them well right away, at least you're doing things that will give you success in the long run.

For example, there are a variety of "one-handed" techniques, where one hand is in charge of putter alignment, and the other assists the stroke in a way that is intended to keep it from affecting that alignment. The "claw" grip is one example.

There is even a variation that Bryson Dechambeau has brought to public attention, where you stand to the side of the putt, face your target, and swing the putter alongside your body. It's an idea that has advantages for putting, but it means doing something different when putting than what you do for every other stroke on the course. Whether the benefits outweigh the drawbacks remains to be determined!

Whatever style you use, the goal is the same: To putt the ball down the intended line of travel, with the intended amount of force. If you are achieving those goals, and making putts, then you are "doing it right".

Standard Two-Handed Technique

Here are the basic elements of the standard two-handed putting technique. I teach it, because it's what I know. But some of the important principles apply to other styles, as well.

- **Palms face each other.**
  If the palms *aren't* facing each other, it's harder to keep the putter head square to the direction of travel, because the arms tend to move in slightly different directions as they come across the body. It's also harder to swing the putter on the intended line. So the tendency is to putt the ball offline, or give it sidespin, or both. Whatever grip you use, the important factor is that your palms face each other. (Personally, I favor a "baseball" grip when putting, and use a interlocking grip for other swings. But that is simply a matter of personal preference.)

- **Eyes over the ball, or just inside.**
  Both systems have strong proponents, and have demonstrated remarkable success. The main thing is that you're not leaning over past the ball, and you're not far away from it. You want your eyes looking down the line of the putt, rather than seeing it at an angle, which can throw off your aim. (Imagine trying to aim a rifle from off to the side. It's a lot harder than sighting down the barrel.) The Putting Practice section in Part IV tells you how to check your alignment and aim.

- **Wrists locked, arms stay straight, and shoulders "rock", creating a pendulum motion.**
  In the old days, some people used a lot of wrist action. But that makes it harder to return the putter face to the ball at just the

right angle to produce topspin, which helps it stick to the green as it rolls. Wrist action reduces consistency, without improving accuracy. Putting from the shoulders creates a long pendulum that sweeps back and through the ball.

- **Size of the backswing is the same as the follow-through.**
  This means you push the putter forward the same amount as you pulled it back. The distance of the backswing then will reliably create the variations in speed when you putt.

- **Size of the swing controls distance.**
  You could try putting with more force for a longer putt and with less force for a shorter one, moving the clubhead the same amount of distance each time. That method requires a lot of feel, and it's difficult to do reliably. An easier technique is to make every putt the "same", at least as far as your timing is concerned. For a longer swing to take the same amount of time, it has to happen faster, which means you are automatically applying more force—but internally, it feels like the same putting action.

- **Weight rests over the forward leg (left leg, for a right-hander).**
  This technique ensures that when you contact the ball your body is in the same position as it is for every other swing you make, which adds consistency. In addition, the weight shift automatically creates a "lean" in the clubshaft, with your hands slightly ahead of the ball and putter head behind it, so the clubshaft is at an angle. The slight lean helps to impart topspin and to keep the ball on the ground, which tends to keep it from popping up at the start of the putt.

  Another way to achieve the same effect is to start with the putter vertical and then begin the putting stroke with a *forward press*—a slight forward movement with the hands that gets the putter shaft leaning, and which also gets the body moving into the stroke.

- **Hips and legs are quiet.**
  Having the weight over the left leg helps to keep both steady. For consistency, you reduce the action to the minimum number of body parts needed to make the putt—the shoulders. For a really

long putt on an over-sized green (see the next point), you may need a bit of twisting action to get the putt to go far enough. But generally, you don't.

- **For a *very* long putt, turn your hips.**
  For a putt that is upwards of 40 or 50 feet—especially when going uphill—you may want to twist your hips and waist on the backswing and when you follow through. That action will greatly reduce your distance-control *precision*, but it will make it possible to cover large distances easily. (*Very* easily. Practice it on the putting green. You'll be surprised by how much farther the ball goes.)

  On average-length putts, you'll be using the "shoulder rocking" technique, with the aim of getting to within at least 3 feet of the hole. For the super-long variety, getting to within 6 feet of the hole is great.

  However, even when your hips are turning, you'll be keeping the putter head on the target line, so the putter is going straight back *from* the target, and straight through *to* the target. (The more twist you add, the more the tendency for a circular swing. But as much as possible, keep the putter head moving down the target line.)

- **Look at the target, keep the image in your head, but keep your eyes on the ball.**
  As you start the putt, consciously visualizing what you just saw helps your mind-body computer do its thing. For a gazillion years, a successful hunt depended on the ability to deliver a projectile to an exact spot. You have that ability. Trust me. Return your eyes to the ball, but keep picturing the hole—especially the size of the hole—because that is your best indicator of distance.

- **Keep your head in place until the ball has left, then tilt and hold.**
  Your head stays still until the ball has left your field of vision or has dropped into the cup. When the ball is gone, *tilt* your head to see where the ball wound up, rather than lifting it, and hold your finish position.

That is the advice given by stars such as Ben Hogan and Tom Watson. Naturally, it is great advice—perhaps the most important tip of all. You keep your body position and your eyes see where the ball finished. The putter is as far forward now at the finish as it was back in your backswing, and your body is holding that position. Your mind-body computer will now correlate the size of your swing with the distance the ball traveled. *You* don't have to do anything but watch. Your body and mind will take care of the rest!

This is another reason for using the distance the putter head travels to control speed, rather than trying to move the putter head faster or slower over a fixed distance. As you watch the ball come to rest, your mind-body computer can associate that exact putter head position with the length of travel. If you vary the force of the putt, your internal computer has to go "back in time" to associate the force of the putt with the ball's final position. It can do it, of course. It has that capability. But it is harder and less consistent.

For more advice on how to putt, check the Recommended Resources for additional sources of instruction. And, as I said at the start, take a lesson. Even take a few!

Direction Control

The importance of good putting mechanics is that they help you make good putts. But there are only three characteristics that make a putt a good one: 1) The putt goes down the line you intended; 2) It goes the distance you intended; 3) It goes down the line it *needed* to go on to get near the hole.

The very first requirement is the ability to putt the ball down the line you intended. To do that, you need to groove in a straight stroke, until it is automatic.

**To get reliable results, the first requirement
is the ability to putt the ball straight.**

There are putting aids you can buy to help acquire this skill, or you can do the drills recommended in the chapter, Learning, Practicing, and Warming Up, but the only real requirement is the ability to keep the putter face square to the target line and move the putter directly down that line with no deviation. Then the ball travels straight down the line, with no argument. It's a matter of physics. It can't do anything else.

Using flat wrists, steady legs and hips, and rocking your shoulders help to make that happen. To groove in the technique, all you need is a series of short, straight putts. If they go straight down the line where you're aiming, you're as good as you need to be.

Once you have the technique, you'll do a few at the start of every session just to warm up and to further groove in that straight stroke. If that is *not* happening, find yourself a putting coach straightaway and diagnose the problem. You can keep reading, keep learning, and keep playing in the meantime. The knowledge and experience you gain will benefit you, eventually. But *until you can putt the ball straight, it will be hard to get reliable results.*

Getting the Right Putter

To practice straight putts, you can practice on the floor at home, find a hole that is on a flat surface, or putt from directly below a hole on a slope, as recommended in the chapter, Learning, Practicing, and Warming Up. That kind of practice gives you direct and immediate feedback on your ability to putt down the line you intend.

If you find that you are consistently missing a straight putt of that kind from 3 or 4 feet away, get yourself a putt training aid like the SKLZ Accelerator Pro putt trainer, or any similar device that will help you groove in a dead-straight stroke. (But watch out, some cheaper models are seriously deficient in the quality department. Try before you buy.)

From 6 or 7 feet away, it's okay to miss a few. But from 3 or 4 feet away, the ball should be going straight in the center of the hole. If you find that you are consistently missing putts of that length on your training device, it may well be that your eyes are not where they need to be! In that case, what appears to you to be a straight line to the hole could be a fraction off.

One great bit of advice I learned early on from one of Jack Nicklaus's instructional books was to make sure my eyes are directly over the ball. When they are, they are also directly over the putter's alignment line, and directly over the line of the putt.

You can check your alignment by holding a plumb-bob next to your eye when you are set up for a putt, or by dropping a ball from your temple. The plumb-bob or ball should touch the ground directly behind the ball (or on it, or in front of it). It should not be closer to you or farther away from you than the ball.

The solution is to adjust the effective length of your putter so that when you address the ball, your eyes are directly over it. That way, you are looking straight down the center of the ball to the alignment line on your putter, and you are *also* looking straight down the line you are aiming on.

You can see a club fitter to get the right combination of shaft length and "lie angle" (the angle at which the shaft leaves the putter head) to make sure that when you're set up, your eyes are directly over the ball.

Or you can take a plumb-bob to a store, and try different putters until you find that one you like—one that "feels right", and that also puts you in the right position. From that position, aligning the center of the putter to the center of the ball won't be a problem—and your aim will improve, as well.

On the other hand, if your head is a little short of the ball, you can simply "choke down" on your current putter to change your head position.

In rare cases, your head may be a little past the ball. If that is the case, and you are already gripping down, you can try taking a higher grip to extend the effective length of the shaft.

Distance Control

When you can putt in a straight line, you have direction control. The next thing you need is distance control: the ability to putt the ball to a given distance.

Raised Alignment Line?

The Cleveland "23.5" putters made a clever adjustment to help you line up the center of the putter with the center of the ball. They raised the alignment line to 23.5 mm above the bottom of the putter head. That lets you keep the putter aligned to the ball, even if your eyes are slightly short of the center, or a little past that point.

But while that arrangement can help you to hit the center of the ball, it can also have the unfortunate effect of giving you a false sense of security, precisely *because* you can line up the ball and putter without having your eyes over the ball.

When your eyes are directly over the ball, they are also directly over the intended line of travel. When your eyes are *not* directly over that line, it's easier to aim slightly off line, without even realizing it.

As you'll see, if you putt straight towards the hole with just the right amount of speed to get there—completely ignoring any slope that moves the ball away from the hole—the ball will always come to rest *directly below the hole*. And that is the easiest putt there is to hole out.

So having precisely the right speed is almost a guaranteed 2-putt. That makes it even more important than having the right line—because if your speed is way off, the ball could wind up almost anywhere, even if the line is close.

To get reliable results, the second (and more important) requirement is the ability to putt the ball to a given distance.

The problem, though, is that distance control is hard! Most everyone finds it difficult, at the start.

Putting to a controlled distance, like music, requires the ability to make small, highly precise movements. Professional musicians spend five hours a day just to *maintain* that kind of precision, and years to acquire the capability.

Professional golfers spend the same kind of time, every single day, to achieve the kind of consistency they need to win.

So accept that it will take time to acquire that skill. Accept it, expect it, and plan for it. And know that every minute you spend practicing to acquire that skill will pay off—in spades. But note, too, that shortly you will have an advantage that will accelerate the process—the ability to get accurate speed feedback from every putt you make.

The exercises in the chapter, Learning, Practicing, and Warming Up, will help you acquire that skill. There are many ways to go about it, but they all boil down to making medium-to-long "lag" putts, and trying to get them within a foot or two of a given target.

One way or another, you'll need to acquire that skill! So in every practice session and every warm-up before a round, spend time grooving in your ability to control distance.

Visualization Skills

To develop distance control in the least possible time, use your visualization skills. Start by noticing that when you stand directly over the cup, it is perfectly round, but when you move away from it, it appears as more of an oval. And the farther away you move, the flatter the oval becomes.

As you look at the cup, take a mental picture. When you return your gaze to the ball, hold that picture in your mind's eye—with special attention to the size of the oval. That visualization will guide your putting strength. And that guide will get better and better if you hold your final position and take feedback from each putt you make.

You will notice, however, if the green is sloping towards you, the cup will appear to be more round. (That's one reason it's helpful to look from a low angle. The closer your eye is to the green, the more accurately the size of the oval reflects the distance to the cup.)

But notice, too, that your *feet* are also very aware of the slope. Even if you weren't consciously aware of it, your internal mind-body computer is. (And now that you know about it, you can be more conscious of it.)

So when you hold the picture in your mind that shows the size of the oval, your mind-body computer is *automatically* adjusting for the slope. Paying conscious attention to the feelings in your feet can speed up the learning process but, again, there is nothing that you have to *do*. You just have to watch, and let your internal computer do the rest.

Given the ability to putt a ball down the intended line, and the ability to putt it for a given distance, the only skill left is the ability to read the green, so you can choose the right line to putt on.

As I mentioned early on, much of that ability derives primarily from the feedback you get from each putt. Once you know how to derive that feedback, your ability will grow from week to week—and even from hole to hole. That is what this book is all about. But first, let's examine the *process* of putting.

The Putting Process

To make great putts and to get great feedback (which will automatically lead to great putts, in time), it helps to follow a consistent process:

1. **Read the green.**
   Get a general sense of the green's slope.

2. **Find the fall line.**
   Find the line on which gravity will pull the ball into the hole.

3. **Judge the break**.
   Get an idea of how much the putt is going to *break* (how far downhill the ball will travel as it moves towards the hole).

4. **Pick a target.**
   Pick a point on that line to aim at—your *target*.

5. **Prepare to putt.**
   - Line up the putt, aiming at your target.
   - Plan to putt with enough force to just "die" the ball at the fall line.
   - If you *really* need to, make a practice stroke.

6. **Keep your head down and make the putt.**
   Don't worry about where the ball is going. You'll find that out in a moment.

7. **Learn from the putt.**
   As the ball leaves your field of vision, tilt your head to see where it finishes.

I've broken things down into multiple parts here, but that's only to bring the bits and pieces into tighter focus. When playing, the "process" is really just three principal steps: **READ** (the first four steps), **PUTT** (the next two), and **LEARN** (the last, and arguably the most important).

1. Read the Green

As Tom Watson points out in Getting Up and Down, you want to be reading the green as you're walking up to it. Gather an overall perspective. What are the general contours of the green? Which way is it sloping?

Recognizing that greens are designed to allow water to drain off, you can make general observations about the terrain. Are there mountains nearby? (Greens will generally slope downhill, the way water wants to go.) Is there a pond, lake, or river nearby? (The green will generally be sloping in that direction.) Are there low areas around the green that can serve as drainage areas? (If there is a metal-grated drain at that location, the green is probably sloping towards it.)

Also, note that holes are generally designed to let water run past a bunker, rather than into it. Take that bit of information into account as you assess the green.

You're not making specific plans at this point. You're just acquiring general information—information that will factor into your plans later. That awareness is so important that master putter Jack Nicklaus once commented that he reads greens he has yet to play whenever his round takes him near them. If the tee box for the 17th hole is near the green for the 18th, he'll be studying the 18th while he's in the teeing area.

As you get closer, you'll begin to acquire more specific information that will help you assess your options. How many levels does it have? Which level is the pin on? Where is your ball?

When you're on the green, ask yourself: Where is water going to flow? That is the key question. The greens are set up to allow rain to flow off. Find that low point (or points). Water anywhere around the hole will be heading there.

Generally, the water will drain directly towards that point. But sometimes, there is an offset. Maybe the water drains towards a collection area in the center of the green, and from *there* it drains off to a river, lake, pond, or drain. Noticing these things will make it easier to take the next step: Finding the fall line.

2. Find the Fall Line

The *fall line* is the direction that things will fall when placed on a slope. The term comes from skiing. It's the fastest, most direct way down any given slope—the direction that gravity takes you, any vaguely round object, or water.

Now you're getting more specific. Because the fall line you're interested in is the one that runs to the hole, as shown in Figure 1.

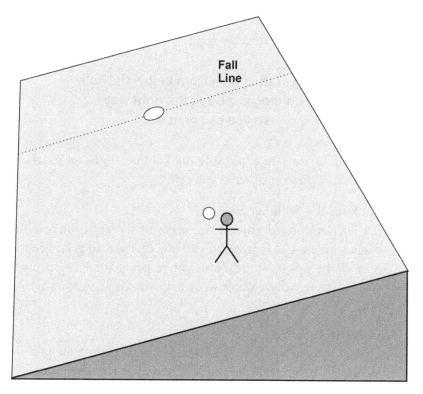

Figure 1: The Fall Line

Find the point on the slope directly above the hole from which water (or a dropped ball) will run directly to the hole, or a point below the hole that runs directly away from it. Those points identify the fall line.

It's important to identify the fall line, because that is the direction from which a ball above the hole will fall into it. A ball on or near the fall line drops into the hole as it comes down the slope. A ball farther away misses the hole. It's that simple.

On a breaking putt, your target will be somewhere on that fall line. We'll get into details later on. But for now, just get used to the idea that finding the fall line is a critical step in the putting process.

The best place to identify the fall line is from below the hole. Why? Because a green is a bit like a book. Looking at the green from above the hole is like looking at only the top edge of the pages with the book upside down. It's pretty difficult to read that way! Looking at it from below the hole is like holding the book the right way up and tilting it towards you, so you can read the page.

> **Looking at the green from below the hole
> is like holding the book the right way up,
> so you can read it.**

There are four ways to determine the fall line. To be an excellent putter, use all of them as often as you can:

1. **Look for the drainage area.**

    Earlier, you looked around the edges of the green to find the place where water is going to run off. That was to get a general idea of the green's slope. Now, you're going to get even more specific, to see where water will run down the slope towards the hole.

2. **Listen to your feet.**

    This is the approach recommended in the AimPoint putting system. The force on your ankles changes as you unconsciously work to stay upright. Becoming aware of those sensations can help to figure out which way the green is running.

3. **Watch your playing partners' putts**.

   Your playing partners can help you a lot more than they intend. And it's not just when they happen to have the same line as you. In fact, the line they're putting on is *irrelevant*. You can use their putts to determine exactly where the fall line is, which is all you really need to know.

   (You might think their putts could tell you something about green speed, but that feedback can only realistically come from your *own* putts—because it is only then that you know how much force was applied. (It is theoretically possible to observe the speed of someone else's ball and see how fast it slows down, but I'm not sure how well we can really do that.)

4. **Watch your own putt**.

   If you are some distance from the hole, and you make a good "lag" putt that is anywhere close to the hole, you can get even more information. Not only do you get an exact read on the break (to find out exactly where the fall line is), but since you know how hard you struck the ball, you also get a great read on green speed. If that first putt comes within a few feet, you have all the information you need to sink the next one.

There are, then, two kinds of putts to observe: yours and your partners'. To watch your partners', find a spot below the hole that looks to be on the fall line. Be sure you are not standing directly in front or behind them, which is a big no-no in golf etiquette. If they are putting from directly above or below the hole, stand a little to the side. Otherwise, standing below the hole stays out of their line and gives you a great read.

You get almost no information when someone else's putt is moving fast. *The most important information is derived when the ball is going slowest*, because that is when the effect of gravity is strongest.

If the ball is moving fast, you can't use it to judge green speed, because you don't really know how hard it was struck. And you can't use it to find the fall line, because early in the putt, the force and angle of the putt is determining the ball's direction. But as the ball comes to rest, gravity has a stronger and stronger effect until, in the last inch or two of travel before it dies, the ball is moving directly down the fall line.

So the tiny "button hook" at the end of an uphill putt, or the small angle at the end of a downhill putt, gives you the precise direction the slope is running—the fall line.

You learn most in the last inch of travel, just before the ball comes to rest.

If the ball is near the hole when it dies, and you are below the hole on the fall line, you'll see the ball coming straight towards you as it comes to rest. If it goes a little to the side of where you're standing, the fall line is over to that side. (If someone else is putting next, you can adjust your position by moving over slightly, to confirm your new read. But once you have a bit of experience with this technique it isn't really necessary to do that.)

The better your playing partners are, the closer the ball will come to the hole, and the better the information you get—but you can generally get some kind of information, no matter who is putting.

Be aware, too, that the direction change at the end of an uphill putt occurs most prominently on a fast, steep green. On a slower, shallower green, the ball will still change direction at the end of its travels, but not as much. On a really slow green, it may not change direction at all. So if a putt *isn't* moving very much at the end, take it as a signal that the green is relatively slow, and there will probably be less break than there appears to be.

As valuable as other people's putts are, you gain even more information from your *own* putts. Acquiring that information is the primary reason you want to tilt your head after the ball leaves your field of vision.

As with your playing partners' putts, the last inch or two of travel before the ball comes to rest tells you exactly where the fall line is. But since you know how much effort went into the putt, you also get a good indication of green speed, and, therefore, a sense of how much break to expect. (The amount of break depends on the combination of green speed and the steepness of the slope. You'll learn more about that in Part II: Putt Feedback.)

The feedback you get will be especially valuable for a lag putt that comes to within 3 feet of the hole. Only the most nefarious pin placements have anything other than a consistent slope for a 3-foot radius around the hole, so if you put the ball anywhere near the hole, your own lag putt gives you a true read of both green speed and the fall line. In other words, it gives you *all the information you need* to make what should be your final putt.

However, to get that feedback, you need to know *precisely* how to evaluate the results you got. Was the putt too fast? Was it too slow? Was it on the right line to start with? Or was it high? Or low? In Part II, you'll learn how to make those determinations with precision.

3. Judge the Break

One of the things that makes golf such a challenge is that greens contain multiple slopes. To putt well, you need the precision of a pool player, but you're doing it on an undulating surface in conditions that change from day to day, and even hour to hour.

When you're facing a green with multiple breaks around the hole, the key question is "Which break dominates the equation?".

Answering that question is the key to finding the fall line. The only good way to do that is to observe the hole from each of the "candidate" locations. This means feeling your feet as you move from one location to the next. Are you moving uphill or downhill? Why is this helpful? Because the point from which everywhere else is *uphill* identifies the real fall line. (I cover this in more detail in the Can't Find the Break part of "Special Situations".)

After you've found the fall line, the next question is how steep is the slope. Your eyes and feet will help you judge that. You'll hone those skills through experience, or you can speed up the process by using a green reader to measure every slope you can find, like the ones listed under Apps and Devices. The more of that you do, the more rapidly you will learn what your eyes and feet are telling you when you are on a given slope.

The final question is how fast is the green. As you'll see, the only way to tell with any certainty is to watch your shots and take feedback from them. Then you have to count on the greens superintendent making the greens consistent from hole to hole.

Once you have a sense of the speed of the green (mostly from previous putts) and a sense of the slope (mostly from your feet), you're in a position to judge how far the ball will *break* on its way to the hole.

Note that break is caused by gravity, and the amount of gravity affecting the putt depends on both the *slope* and the *speed* of a green. So a faster green breaks more than a slower one, just as a steeper slope breaks more than a flatter one.

Also, the force of gravity is effectively a constant for a given slope, which means that the farther you are from the hole, the more the putt will break. So expect more break for a long putt, less break for a short one.

4. Pick a Target

Once you've found the fall line, it's time to pick the *target* for your putt—a point on the fall line above the hole that you will aim at.

After all, you can't putt a curve ball, the way a baseball pitcher does. All you can do is putt in a straight line. After that, it's gravity and the slope of the green that curves the ball into the hole.

From behind your ball, you already have a *sight line* (the straight route from ball to hole), as shown in Figure 2. On a flat green, that is the line you putt on.

But if there is any slope, you will need to find a line to putt on that is higher than the sight line. The goal is to determine how much higher to aim, or how much "rise" to add to the line to offset the "fall" that is going to occur as the ball runs toward the hole. (Finding that target is something of a mystery right now. I know. But you're going to find it much easier to do as you progress through this book.)

To pick your target, visualize the fall line as it runs down the slope to the hole, find a point on that line that has the perfect amount of rise, and take aim at that target.

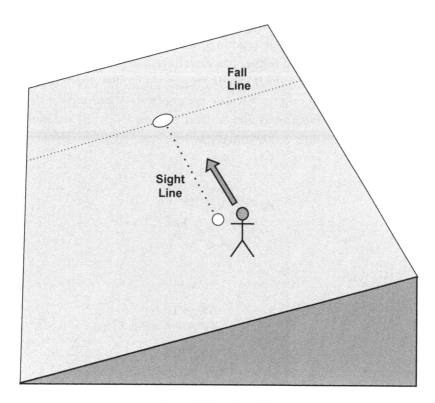

Figure 2: The Sight Line

On a flat surface, as already mentioned, your target is the cup. On a slight slope, your target may be the edge of the cup, or a little inside the edge. On a steeper slope, the target will be a little higher than that. On a steep slope with a fast green, your target may be *much* higher.

> **Pick a point on the fall line that has the
> perfect amount of rise for your putt,
> and take aim at that target.**

The AimPoint system has charts showing that for some distances on some greens you may be aiming as much as 17 *feet* above the hole. (It's no wonder that we amateurs tend to miss on the low side. When was the last time you allowed for 17 feet of break?) But just so you know: Those are the kinds of greens the pros play on. Thankfully, the greens we amateurs play on tend to be a lot more forgiving.

Once you've picked a target, you now have a *target line*, as shown in Figure 3. In practice, the target line is generally called *the line*, as in "finding the line" to putt on, because the entire art of putting consists of finding the right line to aim at, and putting with just the right speed, so the ball arcs gently into the hole.

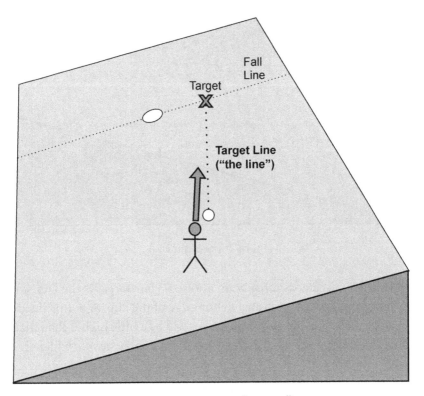

Figure 3: Target Line ("the line")

The ideal target depends on your distance from the hole, the speed of the green, and the slope. Given the many different factors that go into finding the right target, it is no wonder that putting is an art. Don't be discouraged if your initial attempts are far off the mark. What you have probably been missing until now, and what this book will give you, is a way to get the *feedback* you need to tell how far off you were, when you get it wrong. With good feedback, you'll find yourself improving in no time.

But you have to start somewhere! So pick a target, aim at it, and stroke your putt.

The best place I've found to pick that target is from just below the *cross line*—a line running through the hole that is perpendicular to the fall line, as shown in Figure 4.

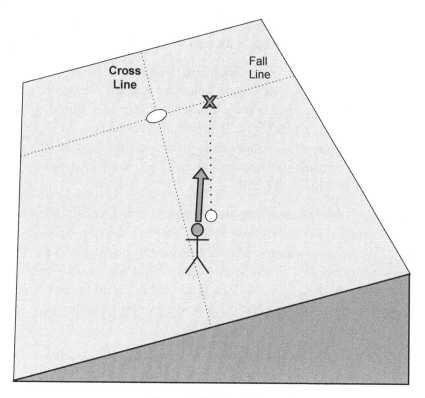

Figure 4: The Cross Line

I go into more detail on the cross line and target line in Part II. But for now, if your ball is near the cross line anyway, just get behind your ball and pick a target. Otherwise, move to a spot near the cross line, at approximately the same distance from the hole as your ball, pick a target, and then move back to your ball.

Visualizing the Arc

Another way to pick a line for your putt is to visualize the arc of the ball as it travels to the hole. Dave Pelz notes that the apex of that arc (the high point) will be one third of the way to the actual target the ball needs to be aimed at. This means if you can visualize the arc, you can pick a point three times higher up the slope than the apex of the ball's arc, and use that as a target to aim at.

In my own experience, I found that two to two-and-a-half times the high point works better for me, but perhaps I have developed a tendency to over-read my putts, allowing for too much break. However, that could be a good sign. It means I am more likely to miss on the "pro" side (the high side), rather than to make an "amateur miss" that goes below the hole.

However, the more important point is that the ability to visualize the arc of the putt still requires a lot of experience. Pelz was an extremely proficient amateur golfer who only lost to the likes of Jack Nicklaus—and only then on the greens. He was good, and he'd had enough experience to see what the ball was going to do after he struck it.

Your ability to visualize the arc of the putt will develop in time, as well. The more putts you see, the better you will get. Couple it with the feedback you get from the putts you have made on the practice green and on the course—feedback you learn how to get in this book—and you have a recipe for success.

You can take the expected arc into account when choosing your target, or not. Your choice. Just know that the most

• • •

important thing is to pick a *target*, because in the end, the only thing you can do is to putt towards that target. After all, you can't throw a curve ball—you can only make a straight putt! So pick a target to aim at, and putt towards that target.

Once you have picked a target, you aim down the *target line*—the line between your ball and your target. That way, you are making what is essentially a straight putt towards your target. Gravity and the slope of the green do the rest, arcing the ball into the hole—but throughout the round, you're doing the exact thing every time—making a straight putt. That's why it is so important to have a target to aim at.

For putts that are 10 feet or less (or for longer putts with a single break) that is pretty much all you'll need to do: Pick a point, aim at it, and putt. Then hold your finish until the ball comes to rest, and observe the results. Your body's natural feedback mechanisms will take care of the rest.

For longer putts, divide the putt into thirds. The third that is closest to the hole is the area where gravity will have the most effect. As Phil Mickelson's caddy Jim Mackay points out in a Golf Digest story, 10 Rules for Reading Greens:

> "Reading putts from behind the hole … provides the most accurate perspective of all because you get a closer look at the last few feet of the ball's route to the hole. The area around the hole is critical: If there's any slope at all, the ball will react to it because it's rolling so slowly."

On the other hand, I'll demonstrate later that you don't actually need to be *behind* the hole to find the ideal target (see "One Target to Rule Them All" in the chapter, Getting a Break). You can get a great perspective from a 90-degree angle. Since you don't have to walk all the way behind the hole, you can take less time to pick your target. But the important point is that it is *the last few feet* of the putt that are most critical, with regard to determining break.

So, having divided the putt into thirds, start by picking a point to aim at, based on the third that is closest to the hole. Then read the middle third. Is there a small hill going the other way? If so, back off from the point you originally picked, but not all the way because that break will count for less. Finally, read the third closest to the ball. Add or subtract an additional amount based on the movement you see there. The effect of gravity will be least in this area, but it will still count for something. Figure that it will be half as much as the effect in the last third, with the middle third somewhere in between.

In the end, you'll wind up with a single point of aim, somewhere on the fall line. That point is a) above the hole, b) right on the fall line, and c) just high enough to counterbalance the effect of gravity.

For a short putt (within 2 feet or so) you don't want to "give away the hole", so pick a spot inside the hole—for example, "inside left edge", or "edge of the hole". That way, if there is less break than you imagined, the ball will still drop into the cup.

For a putt that has more break, you could measure in terms of balls, such as, "one ball outside", or "3 balls". For medium breaks, you might instead think in terms of feet—"a foot away", "2 feet away". For larger breaks, try club lengths—"a club", "a club and a half".

Or you could be more intuitive about it, and simply see a spot on the fall line that looks about right. The distance measurements are helpful when a caddie, say, is trying to communicate his read to his player. You may find them useful if you talk to yourself. (Or not.)

Putting is an art, after all. In the end, you always wind up using your intuition—a fancy word for the results of sophisticated calculations done behind the scenes by your mind-body computer, based on past experience, which comes to your awareness as a "gut feel".

Acquiring the right feedback from each putt is the key to training that computer system. In Part II, you'll find out how to fine-tune the feedback process so that it is very exact. For now, you just need to understand that if you pick the right point to aim at, and you putt the ball with the right amount of force, the ball will end up in the hole, every single time.

Two things to remember here: 1) A putt anywhere *near* the ideal target will leave a very makeable second putt—especially with the information you'll have acquired from the first one; 2) The goal is *progress*, not *perfection*.

5. Prepare to Putt

All the mental preparation is done. It's time to step up to the putt and stroke it.

Take Aim

Once I've picked a target to aim at, I like to set my putter down so the edge of the face is pointing to that spot. That is a good time to pick a *near target*—a point 4 to 6 inches ahead of the ball that is in line with the target, that you intend the ball to roll over on as it starts its journey.

Holding the putter in that position as you move around to the side is a little awkward, but it works. Once you get your feet square to the putter, they're square to the intended line. You can then flip the blade so it is perpendicular to your stance, and therefore square to that line.

On the other hand, if you picked a near target, you can be more relaxed about it. Keep your gaze on the intermediate target as you step up to the ball, and aim the putter at it. As the saying goes, "Every putt is a straight putt, for the first 6 inches." So that method works rather well for the ball to get started on the right line.

If you have a marker on the ground, and a line on the ball, you can also position the ball so the line on it is going down the target line. That technique works best if you have identified an intermediate aiming point because, when you get down to position your ball, it becomes harder to see a far-away target clearly. (It also takes extra time, so that technique is best used when you *already* have a marker on the ground.)

Whatever method works for you, do it. What's important is the goal: To get yourself set up to putt along the line you've chosen.

Once you're set up, gaze at your target for three seconds or so, and visualize that point as you address the ball. Studies of basketball players have shown that performance improves dramatically when their eyes are locked on the rim for three to five seconds before they pull the trigger. The same thing can work for you. (Important: Gaze at the *target*. That's the important thing. The hole will take care of itself.)

In *Optimal Putting*, Geoff Mangum points out that your internal awareness of the angle of your neck is one of the ways you know how far away you are from your target. Gazing at the target for three seconds gives your internal computer time to register that sensation.

Those few seconds also give your mind-body computer a chance to gauge the amount of effort needed to put the ball where you want it. The mind-body computer is a remarkably effective piece of equipment. Give it a chance to do its thing, and remember to tilt your head to watch the results as you hold the putter in its finishing position. Your natural learning instincts will take care of the rest.

Visualize "the Force"

As you gaze at your target, imagine how much of a stroke it will take to reach the fall line. Your mind-body computer will do the rest. (I'll explain why in the next chapter, and cover the few exceptions.)

In general, putt with just enough force to reach the fall line.

Of course, the amount of force you need depends on the angle you're putting up the hill, the speed of the green, and the steepness of the slope. That's a lot to take into account!

That is where feedback comes in. There are highly accurate calculations that *could* be made, once you know the precise distance, the degree of slope, the actual green speed, and your putting angle. But calculations like that do you little good on the course!

What you need to develop instead is an intuitive *feel* for how hard to stroke the putt, to get the ball to the hole from *this* angle, on *that* slope. But to do that, you have to be able to separate feedback on your *read* from feedback on your *speed*—things you'll be learning shortly.

That is where practice comes in, too. Once you can putt in a straight line and can control your distance on the practice green, you have all the skills you need. It's just a matter of honing them.

Return to "Center"

When you finish looking at your target, return your gaze to the ball, or to the near target in front of it. At that point, hold for a second or so and, in your mind's eye, *see* the fall line target. (You can also be aware of the hole, since the shape of the oval you see tells you how far away you are, as mentioned earlier.)

Another delightful tip from *Optimal Putting* is the idea that the time it takes for your head to swivel back to center *also* factors into your sense of distance. Magnum also mentions that it takes a moment for the fluid in your inner ear to settle.

The online PDF also explains that it is helpful to "wait for the shine on the ball", before pulling the trigger:

"Looking down to the ball, the eyes will also have to adjust the lenses to focus on this new distance (closer than the target) .... In adults, this process takes about a full second, so the shine on the ball's cover will come into sharper focus as you are looking at it. Just wait in patient stillness as vision and balance reset themselves. This step clears the mind and sets the pivot and eyes in a stable position for the stroke."

So holding a steady gaze in the "center" position achieves several goals:

1. You register the time it took to turn your head.
2. You re-establish your inner equilibrium.
3. Your zero in your optical focus.
4. You "center yourself"—relaxing and expanding your awareness before stroking the putt.

When you make your stroke to your chosen target, you will automatically add force to compensate for the amount of uphill. That's perfect. The force you add for the uphill counteracts the pull of gravity downhill. What's left is the exact amount of force needed to reach the hole. (A more exact explanation is coming in the next chapter. For now, just go with it.)

The idea, then, is to putt with just enough force so that, when it is directed towards the spot you picked on the fall line, the ball dies at the hole. If you do that, and you picked the right spot, the ball goes in. But if you missed (who doesn't?), you take the feedback from that putt and use the information on the next one.

Practice Stroke?

I used to take a practice stroke from behind the ball. Or sometimes I would take one from beside it. Both seem to work pretty well, but I never did figure out which method I liked best. What I did learn is that if you're going to take a practice stroke, *one is plenty*. It tells your muscles what to do. Do it twice, and your muscles get confused. Only do it a second time if you're *sure* the first was wrong. Otherwise, better to just make the putt and take feedback from it.

Nowadays, on short- and medium-length putts, I usually don't make any practice stroke at all—because for most putts a practice stroke is *totally unnecessary*. It's like tossing a small ball to a child in the park. You don't take "practice swings" with your arm. Your hand-eye coordination is a heck of a lot better than that. You just focus your gaze on the target, and toss the ball. (Tour players do the same thing when they toss the ball to their caddies. No practice swing needed!)

The same principle works in putting. Once you pick your line and aim at the point you've selected, you just need to pull the trigger. No practice stroke needed. After you putt, simply take your feedback, as you learn how to do in this book. If it was too hard or too soft, just make note of the fact. Your internal computer will do the rest of the work, and automatically adjust for the next time.

For most putts, a practice stroke isn't necessary.

If more people understood this principle, a round would take a lot less time!

There is one exception to that rule, though: If you scuff the ground on a putt, and leave the ball woefully short as a result, take it as a sign that, in essence, you "forgot where the ground is". If you can, take a couple of practice strokes before you leave the green, to find it again. And on the next green, take a practice stroke just to be *sure* you found it.

Note, too, that is useful to take a practice stroke when chipping, to get a feel for how much resistance the club will encounter, and to get a feel for where the club meets the ground, on an uneven lie. But *there is no resistance on a putt, so when the swing is relatively short, a practice stroke is generally unnecessary.*

For a long putt that requires a larger swing, especially one that requires a hip turn, it can be useful to make a practice swing, in order to dial in your body motion. But for anything shorter than that, forget about it!

You Will Learn—You Can't Help It

I once knew a terrific athlete named Joe Battalia who was recruited for the US National volleyball team by none other than volleyball superstar Karch Kiraly. Joe was flattered, but replied that he had never played volleyball in his life. "Not to worry", replied Karch, "We practice six hours a day. You get good at it. It's what human beings do!"

And that is the important point. Over a lifetime of playing and practice, you will spend at least as many hours putting as a fellow like Joe spent playing volleyball for the two or three years he was on the team. You will, quite simply, get good at it.

Learning to read greens and take the right feedback from your putts will help you get much better, much faster. But the main thing is that you don't need to stress about it. It's going to happen. But it is going to take time. Practice strokes before you putt won't speed up the process!

Double Exhale to Relax

One of the hardest things to learn in the golf swing is the feeling of totally relaxed forearms, with no tension in the grip, so you are swinging the club with your body, rather than with your hands.

The trick is keep the grip just tight enough to prevent twisting, but loose enough that the club could still be pulled out of your hands.

One way I've found to get the feeling is to jam the club under a piece of furniture. Then practice gripping the club with just enough pressure that your hands won't turn, but you can still pull them slowly off the club. It's tricky! And it does turn out to be the same amount of pressure you would use to hold a baby bird.

To maintain that degree of pressure, you need to relax your forearms. To promote that relaxation, you can use the tip that Sir Nick Faldo has tried to pass on a couple of times, during televised games. I call it the *double exhale*. It's simple really. After exhaling once, you exhale a second time. Something about doing that is just deeply, totally relaxing.

You're focusing on your forearms, of course, but your entire body relaxes in the process, which does wonders for your swing—so it is a great anti-tension device. (Unfortunately, in the limited time Faldo has to explain the concept between televised shots, it sounds like a breathing practice where you continuously exhale, without ever inhaling! Because it sounds impossible, it's easy to set the idea aside before discovering its benefits.)

6. Keep Your Head Down and Make the Putt

"Watch the ball disappear" is some of the best advice I ever got. Gazing at the ball (or your near target, just ahead of it) keeps your head steady.

The trick is to keep the ball or blade of grass at the exact same spot in your field of vision and make sure it stays the same size. If you do, then your head and shoulders are not moving closer to it or away from it—because where your head goes, your shoulders follow.

Depending on where you have chosen to gaze, then either:

- **Watch the ball disappear**, or

- **Watch the ball roll over your near target**

Either technique keeps your head steady for the duration of the stroke, reducing the tendency to scuff the ground or "top" the ball.

As you will have noticed, I have emphasized getting feedback as the key to improving your putting game, so you do have to move your head a little—but only by tilting it. (That movement is explained more fully in the next point.)

The Secret of Formation Flying

In formation flying, you have to stay right on the wing of another airplane. To do that, you center your gaze on its wing. You're aware of everything else in your field of vision, but you keep the center of focus right there on the wing. Then you adjust your speed and direction to keep it in the same spot in your field of vision (so it doesn't drift off), and to keep it the same size (so it isn't getting closer or farther away). This is exactly the same principle as "watching the ball disappear" when putting.

I practice this when going through an intersection after the light turns green. I center my gaze on the bumper ahead of me and stay a fixed distance behind it—while at the same time being aware of the flow of traffic ahead, and all the time being on the alert for brake lights. Effectively, I am "formation flying" in my car, while traveling at a slow rate of speed. You'll find—however and wherever you practice it—that this same visual process will be helpful when putting. And it's great for your other golf swings, as well.

7. *Learn* from the Putt

By now, you have picked up that the most important step for improving your putting is to *learn* from the putt you just made. You want to know if you had the right line and the right speed. If you had both, of course, you'll have made the putt. But assuming you didn't, *you need to know what correction to make.* That is the crux of the matter, and the real point of this book. It's so important that it takes up several chapters in Part II.

The first thing you'll observe is how close the ball comes to your near target—the one 4 to 6 inches ahead of the ball. If you're gazing at the ball, you'll monitor that point with your peripheral vision. If you're already gazing at it, you'll watch as the ball rolls over it.

That step gives you feedback about putt *direction.* The next step gives you even more vital feedback about putt *speed*, and the quality of your *read*.

To do that, it is especially important to watch the ball as it comes to rest. As mentioned earlier, the last inch of the putt gives you the most valuable information you can get about the slope of the green—*especially* on a fast green.

On a slow green or shallow slope, a putt is more likely to hold its original line right to the end. But for any significant slope and green speed, *you learn the most from the last inch of travel, because that part of the putt shows you the true fall line*, dispelling any optical illusions or misreads you may have been prone to.

You learn the most from the last inch of travel, because that part of the putt shows you the true fall line.

The length of the putt, meanwhile, tells you how far the ball rolls for a given amount of force. Knowing that, your mind-body computer will make the appropriate adjustment.

The best way to get that feedback is simply to *tilt your head* (rather than lifting it) and *hold your final position*, as recommended by Tom Watson in Getting Up and Down. Tilting your head lets you see where the ball finishes, without changing your body position. Keeping your body in that position makes it easier for your mind-body computer to associate the size of the putt with the distance the ball travels.

So after the ball leaves your field of vision, tilt your head to watch it, and hold that position until it comes to rest. Do that, and your speed of improvement will increase considerably.

Now, before we get on to the nitty-gritty of how to get useful feedback, I want to quickly address the two types of putting philosophies you are likely to come across: the "power putt" and "die at the hole".

Putting Philosophies

There are two theories on putting: the "power putt" philosophy, which aims to take break out of the equation as much as possible, and the "die at the hole" philosophy, which tries to have the ball running out of speed as it gets to the cup.

This chapter compares those philosophies. As you'll see, each has its place.

"Power Putt" vs. "Die at the Hole"

The power putt theory says you should ram the ball into the back of the cup. That stroke minimizes break, so it's great for short putts, when there isn't too much break to start with.

The other approach to putting is for the ball to be slowing down so much that it is nearly at a standstill when it falls into the cup—dying at the hole. This method is not quite as reliable for short putts, but those make up only a fraction of the putts you face.

It does give you a better chance of making breaking putts though, mostly because with every putt, you are practicing your ability to putt to a specific distance—and that style of putting gives you better feedback on green speed and your distances, as you'll see in Part II.

If every putt gives you precise feedback on your putting speed, your sense of how hard to putt will improve throughout the round. Then, when you face a breaking putt, your chances of success will be that much better.

There are also the cases where the hole is at the edge of a "shelf", with a drop off behind it. The only way to get near this kind of hole without plunging past it is to control your speed. So every putt that gave you precise feedback on putting speed will pay dividends.

In addition, there are times when the hole is below the shelf. In that situation (described in more detail in Part III), you need to putt just barely to the edge of a shelf, allowing gravity to take the ball the rest of the way to the hole. Pretty much the only way to make that kind of putt is with precise speed, so the ball just barely topples over the edge.

In general, a power putter will make more straight putts, if only because they don't come up short as often. And they will do well on short putts with little break, because they effectively take the break out of the equation. But on every other kind of putt, they tend to do less well than a die-at-the-hole putter.

Most of the time, then, the die-at-the-hole approach is preferable. But the power-putt philosophy does make sense when you're below the hole, near the fall line, and not too far away (say, 3 feet or so). In that situation, you take the curve out of the equation, and give yourself what amounts to a straight putt. Your odds of making it will increase, and a miss won't hurt you too badly. (I'll have more to say on that subject in the upcoming section "How Much Does Excess Speed Hurt?".)

But when you're *not* near the fall line below the hole, the power-putt philosophy reveals its weaknesses. Taking the curve out of the equation in that situation means you need to putt on a lower line to hole the putt. But then:

1. If you miss, you have a longer comeback putt, aiding and abetting the slope's "inclination" (pun!) to take you away from the hole.

2. When you're putting downhill, the uphill side of the cup can act like a ramp, making it easier for the ball to shoot over the cup, even if the putt is on line.

When a die-at-the-hole putt misses, on the other hand, it tends to come to rest directly below the hole, leaving a straight uphill putt coming back. And as we discuss next, that kind of putt is the easiest putt there is to make.

Uphill Putts Are Easiest

One reason that the die-at-the-hole philosophy is so successful is that it leaves you with more second putts from below the hole. The reason: A putt that underestimates the break played with perfect speed always stops directly below the hole, as you'll see demonstrated in the chapter, The Science of Breaking Putts. And uphill putts are the easiest kind there are to make, for several reasons.

Probably the most important reason is that the raised lip at the back of the cup acts as a backstop. Gravity, being the unrelenting force that is, causes the ball to begin dropping the moment it goes over the edge of the cup.

From above the hole, the raised lip acts like Evel Knievel's ramp. It helps a fast ball shoot over the hole. But from below, that lip is a backstop that stops a fast ball dead in its tracks, so it drops into the hole. (It is possible to strike the ball *so* hard that it hits the backstop and bounces back over the hole. But it takes a mighty propulsion to do that.)

Because of the backstop, there are more speeds at which the ball will fall into the hole. So when you are near the fall line below the hole, a fast putt on a shallow line (one that has less arc) is as likely to drop as a slower putt on the "perfect" line (an arcing putt where the ball tip-toes into the hole just as it is coming to rest). In fact, it is *more* likely, since there is little chance of coming up short.

In addition to having a wider range of successful speeds, there is also the fact that the ball can enter the hole from more angles. We'll be discussing this factor in greater detail at the end of the Fine Tuning chapter, in the section, "The Ideal Entry Point" but the gist is this:

- From near the fall line *above* the hole, the ball can enter only from the top half of the hole.

- But from below the hole, the ball can barrel in from the bottom, slide in from either side, or trickle in from the top. In fact, from below the hole near the fall line, the ball can conceivably drop from nearly any angle at all—a 360-degree circumference of possible entry points.

In short, from below the hole there is a wide range of angles and speeds at which the ball will drop, and a backstop to help. It's no wonder that uphill putts are the easiest kind to make.

How Much Does Excess Speed Hurt?

When you're putting uphill, gravity is acting on the ball the whole way. For any reasonable speed, a miss will tend to come to rest near the hole. On the other hand, going downhill on a fast green, what seems like a reasonable speed can take you far past the hole.

The question is: How *much* does excess speed hurt when you're going downhill? To answer that question, you can perform the same experiment I did. (If you aren't interested in the experiment, you can skip to my conclusions in the last paragraph of this section.)

I took my trusty Green Speed Reader to my local short game practice area. I tested the green speed, and found it be running between 7 and 8 on the StimpMeter. Then I found a hole on a slope. My BreakMaster slope reader told me it was about a 4-degree slope (pretty steep). (You'll find out more about the measuring devices later on.)

That was my test hole. It was more steep than you will find on a typical course, but the green was about average speed—so a fast green would have similar characteristics, even for a greatly reduced slope.

I put the ball about halfway up the ramp on the Green Speed Reader, and found a spot below the hole where the ball just rolled into the hole. The spot was about 20 inches away. I moved the ramp over a few inches to miss the hole, and put the ball at the top of the ramp, doubling the speed of the putt. The result: The ball went about 10 inches farther.

Since the hole is 4 inches across, that meant the ball went about 6 inches past the hole. Not bad, for a double-speed putt! Anything between trickle-in speed and double that would clearly work just fine, so there is a decent margin of error for an uphill putt.

The next step was to put the ball above the hole, and find the position where a half-ramp roll would just make it to the hole. I started about 2 feet from the hole, but I knew the ball would go farther, so I started a few inches away from the fall line, to get an indication of how much farther I would need to move back to find that position.

I put the ball halfway up the ramp, and let it go. To my surprise, it raced by the hole, and went some 8 *feet* beyond it. Not inches. *Feet.* And the green was leveling out at that point. Clearly, even half of the original speed wouldn't have been close. In fact, the fraction needed would have been too small to measure! There was no point in going further, so I concluded the experiment right there.

The moral was clear: While it makes sense to be aggressive going uphill, it makes *zero* sense to be aggressive going downhill—if you miss, you will massively overshoot. To stay close to the hole with any kind of downward slope and/or green speed, you *really* need to control your pace. As a putt moves away from being directly uphill, the less sensible it is to make a strong putt.

Summary

You *can* choose a flatter line and putt with more speed to hole a putt. Doing so may even increase your probability of making that shot. But at the same time, you reduce your chances of getting good feedback on green speed, and of landing directly below the hole if you miss, where even a 4- or 5-footer is very makeable.

Choosing a flatter line is a good option on, say, an uphill 3-footer that you really should make. That way, the back of the hole acts as a backstop, and extra speed doesn't hurt very much on a miss.

For a longer putt, or anywhere other than below the hole near the fall line, aim on a higher line where the ball dies as it gets to the hole. (Finding that line will be the subject of Part II, next.)

Part II

///

Putt Feedback

THIS SECTION TELLS YOU how to understand *exactly* what's happening when you make a breaking putt—or even when you see one. That feedback is the *key* to mastering the greens.

The Science of
Breaking Putts

The preceding chapters covered putting basics and the putting process. Next, we're going to begin covering genuinely new ground: How to evaluate your putt to get the feedback you need to improve both your next putt and your entire game.

To learn from your putt, you need to be able to answer two important questions:

1. Did I have the right *read*?

2. Did I have the right *speed*?

This means you're going to need to evaluate the results of each putt with respect to two factors: *speed* and *line*. Once you understand exactly how to do that, you'll find that you know exactly what is happening on the greens. Mystery solved!

As you begin digesting that feedback, your ability to pick the right line will rapidly improve. And your ability to putt with the right pace will improve dramatically in time—because in each case you will know what corrections you need to make!

Note:

If you just want to know the rules that tell you how to evaluate a putt, you can skip to the Summary at the end of Part II (page 131). That chapter will tell you what you need to know. Knowing the

73

rules will help your game, but the greens will still be a mystery! So come back here when you're done, to understand *why* the principles work.

The basis for the model I'm presenting here is a concept from physics: the *vector*. (Okay, it *is* a concept that's used in rocket science, but it's a really simple one, especially as it applies here. And understanding it makes a world of difference.)

In this chapter, you learn what vectors are and how they work. You also learn how to understand exactly what happened to each and every putt—both the ones you see, and the ones you make yourself. In the following chapters, you will find out how to evaluate those putts—in other words, how to tell in very exact terms whether the line or speed (or both) of the putt was off, and by how much.

The goal of this chapter is to give you the background information you need to understand the next two. So bear with the discussion for a while. It won't take long, and it won't be hard. If you just follow along and understand the main concepts, you'll be well-prepared for the material that follows.

Understanding Vectors

A *vector* is an arrow that depicts both a *force* and a *direction*. The amount of force is shown by its length. While the arrow's direction, as you'd guess, shows the direction of the putt—in other words, the direction in which the force is applied. Super simple.

Figure 5 shows you what vectors look like. Let's say you putt towards a hole on a flat green. Three of the many possible outcomes are depicted in the diagram as vectors: One where the putt goes too short and to the left; one too long and to the right; and one where you putt with the perfect amount of force, right to the hole. The diagram shows what each of those putts looks like when drawn as a vector.

If we think about putting mechanics, the first goal is to putt the ball towards the target you're aiming at (get the line or direction right), while the second goal is to putt with the right amount of force to reach the target (get the speed or distance right). In other words, the *line* and *speed* components of a putt correspond exactly to the *direction* and *force* components of a vector.

Comprehensive Keys to the Green uses vector analysis to explain how to tell which of these two components (or both) was off when you miss a putt and in each case, by how much. Once you have that information, your mind-body will automatically adjust itself.

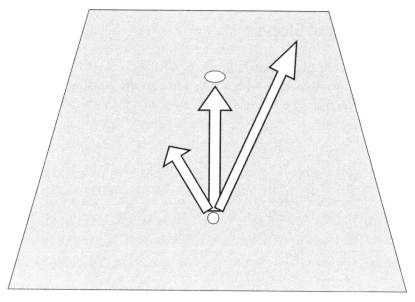

Figure 5: Putt Vectors: Short Left, In, Long Right

On a flat green, those vectors are easy to see. In each case, the ball's starting position is at the start of the vector-arrow, and its finishing position is at the end—so the vector displays the ball's exact path and final position. On a breaking putt, things are a little harder to visualize. But as you'll see, the length of the arrow and its direction are the key to determining where the ball winds up. To start that analysis we'll look at the effect of gravity and the slope of the green.

First, though, let me set your mind at rest: You will *not* be doing some sort of complicated vector analysis to line up a putt! You won't even be doing a vector analysis to evaluate the results of your putt. No. The vector analysis is just a tool for *understanding*.

I'm using that tool to explain *why* the information I'm giving you is correct and believable. When you are on the course and on the practice green, things are a lot simpler: You only need to see where the ball wound up to understand *exactly* what happened, with respect to both distance and direction. By the time you get to the end of Part II, you'll know precisely how to do that, and you'll understand why it works.

The Effect of Slope

Of course, none of us has ever met a totally flat green—there is always a pesky slope. The slope adds a new force to the equation—gravity. That force can also be represented by a vector, as shown in Figure 6.

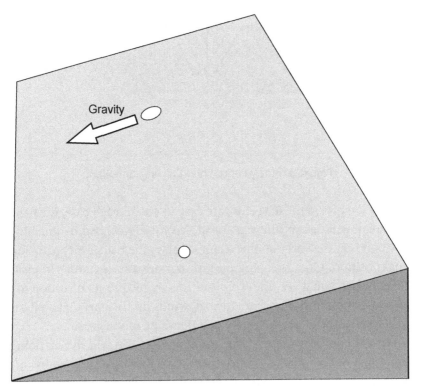

Figure 6: The Gravity Vector

When you add in the gravity vector of the slope to the original "flat" putt, you get a new vector, which shows where the putt on the sloped green will end up. To see where the ball winds up when there are two vectors at work, you "combine" them by placing them end to end, and then complete the triangle, as in Figure 7.

Figure 7 shows what happens if you putt straight towards the hole with just the right amount of speed (force) to get there if the green were flat, completely ignoring any break the green might have. In that case, the ball always comes to rest directly below the hole.

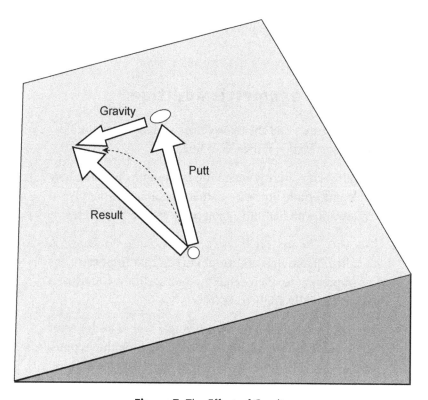

Figure 7: The Effect of Gravity

Intuitively, you can see how it works. If the slope is shallow, the gravity vector will be short, and the ball is deflected only slightly. But if the slope is steep, the ball winds up farther away from the hole—and would be reflected by a longer gravity vector. The *result vector* is what you get after combining the two.

You can prove this for yourself, with a ramp to roll the ball with consistent speed and (ideally) a green you can tilt to control the slope. To do the experiment, you find a position from which you can see that a ball rolling down the ramp goes to the hole when the surface is flat. Then you tilt the surface, and watch the ball come to rest directly below the hole. But while it isn't difficult to get a ramp—see the Recommended Resources—a tilting surface is a lot harder to find! (Dave Pelz built himself one. If you're ever in one of his facilities, try the experiment. Later, I'll have some experiments you can do yourself, without having to build a tilting green.)

Geometric Addition

Figure 7 shows that the two vectors add together, but they add *geometrically*, rather than linearly.

(If both vectors were going in the exact same direction, they would indeed add linearly—as many a golfer who has turned a missed downhiller into a long come-backer will attest.)

This isn't Theoretical Physics 101, though. So knowing it's called "geometric addition" isn't all that important. It's just important to realize that the 1+2 addition you're used to doesn't really apply to vectors.

Instead, you're dealing with a triangle where each vector is one side, and the result of adding them is the hypotenuse of the triangle—whose length obviously depends on the angle between the vectors.

This book isn't about physics, though. It's about putting—and there is a *very* important point to be made: If you're on a slope, and putt the ball towards the hole with just enough force to reach it on a flat green, the ball winds up *directly below the hole*, at a distance determined by the force of gravity. Always!

**If you putt the ball directly towards the hole,
with just enough force to reach it,
the ball always winds up *directly below* the hole.**

And that is another reason for preferring the die at the hole putting strategy. When you putt with perfect speed, your next putt is the easiest one there is to make—straight uphill. If you made a power putt, and you missed, the come-backer is made more difficult by exactly the degree to which you powered past the hole.

Of course, the path that the ball actually travels is curved, as shown by the dotted line in Figure 7. That's because the speed of the putt is strongest when the putt starts out, so it has a greater effect than gravity. But by the end of the putt, the force of the original stroke is negligible, so it is gravity that is exerting the strongest force.

In short, the ball *starts* in the direction you choose, but it *finishes* in the direction gravity chooses. That's why it's so helpful to watch putts as they die. The last inch or two of travel tells you *exactly* which way gravity is working.

The 2-Dimensional Putting Plane

As you've seen, two force vectors—such as your putt and gravity—can be added together to produce a result vector, the end of which shows where the ball stops. But it works the other way, as well.

Any vector in a plane (in our case, the green) can be broken down into *component* vectors, with each component running along one axis of the plane. So with an X-axis and Y-axis, any given vector can be broken down into its X and Y components, as shown in Figure 8.

In the example shown in Figure 8, you'll notice that the X-axis component is longer than the Y-axis component, but neither is quite as long as the original force vector. The sum of the two components can be viewed as the long side (the hypotenuse) of a right-angle triangle, as Figure 9 shows.

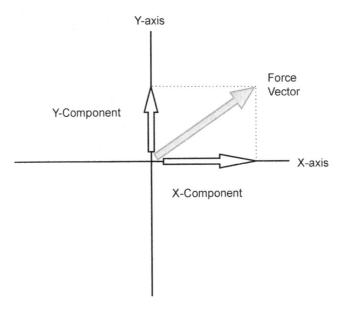

Figure 8: Component Vectors on an X-Axis and Y-Axis

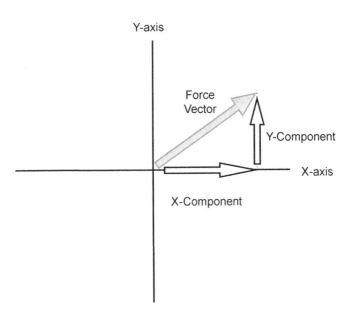

Figure 9: Component Vectors as a Triangle

In other words, the two component vectors can be placed "end to end"—the same way we previously combined the gravity and putt vectors.

Great, you're thinking, I'm reliving high school physics lessons! But what I'm going to show is how this kind of analytical system makes it possible to easily and quickly improve how we read greens and get feedback from our putts. Without some solid basis, we are stuck using the same faulty "intuition" that produces our 3-putts!

The important thing to recognize, when it comes to putting, is that the influence of gravity creates one axis that runs through the hole. That *gravity axis* you will recognize as none other than the fall line. The other axis is a line running through the hole that is perpendicular to the gravity axis. We'll call that perpendicular axis the *cross line*. If the ball happens to be on that line, we can also call it the *sight line* from the hole to the ball (see Figure 10).

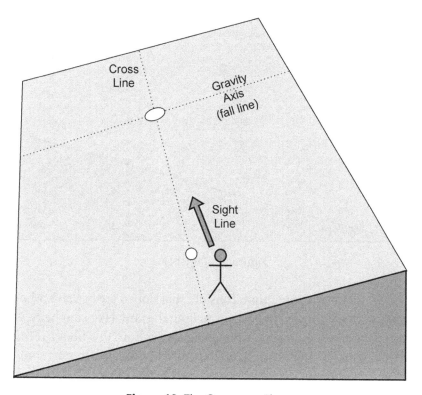

Figure 10: The Green as a Plane

But here's the thing: On any breaking putt, the sight line that goes to the hole is deceiving! You want to ignore that line, and focus on the *target line*: the line that goes from your ball to your *target*, which will turn out to be a point of aim on the fall line, as shown in Figure 11.

After putting, your focus will include the sight line, because it will give you important feedback you need to keep improving your putts. But *before* you putt, your focus is totally on the target line.

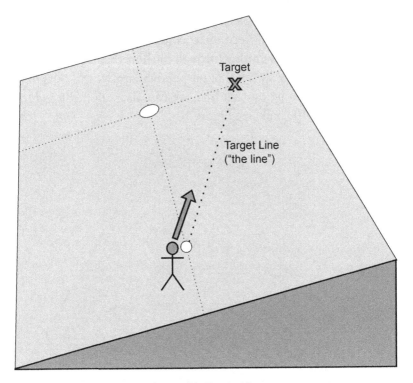

Figure 11: Target Line

With that concept in mind, consider that sloped green again, where gravity adds a downward pull throughout the putt. (For simplicity, we assume a constant angle on the plane throughout this book. Things are obviously a bit more difficult in reality, but we have to start somewhere—and the understanding you gain here will pay big dividends, even when the putting surface has multiple angles.)

Any putt you make can be represented by a vector, and that *putt vector* can be broken down into two component vectors: the amount of force headed towards the gravity axis (the *horizontal* component), and the amount of force directed uphill along the gravity axis (the *vertical* component).

Figure 12 shows the forces acting on the ball (the putt and gravity) as gray arrows. The white arrows show the horizontal and vertical components of the putt.

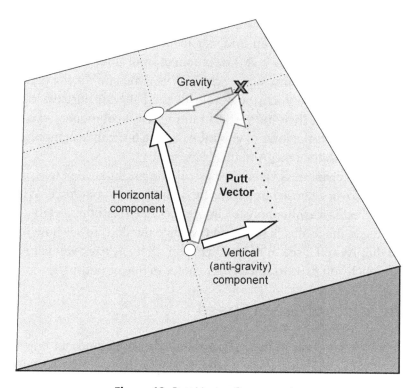

Figure 12: Putt Vector Components

In this case, the diagram shows the components of a *perfect* putt—one in which the horizontal component has the exact amount of force needed to sink the ball on a flat surface, while the vertical component has the exact amount needed to compensate for gravity. The resulting *putt vector* will sink the ball, every single time.

This is an experiment you can do for yourself, on any green that has a slope. Find a spot on the green where you can use the ramp to roll the ball into the hole time after time. All you need to do is keep the ramp pointed in the same direction, and start the ball from the same height on the ramp. Change either one by very much, and the ball starts missing.

Of course, a steeper slope has a bigger gravitational vector, so you have to aim higher. A shallower slope, on the other hand, has a smaller gravitational vector, so you allow for less "break". (Break is the distance the ball is going to slide downhill as a result of gravity.)

At this point, then, you understand in very exact terms what a "perfect putt" really is. It is the combination of direction and force that has the right component vectors. When you aim for the perfect target on the gravity axis, and you hit the ball with just the right amount of force, then the vertical (anti-gravity) component exactly counterbalances the force of gravity, while the horizontal component gets the ball to the hole. And that is the goal!

Previous chapters covered the basic putting skills needed to stroke the ball down a chosen line with the desired amount of force. What comes next is learning how to choose that line (read the green) and how to get the feedback you need (evaluate the putt) to see how well you did. As you'll see in the next chapter, that feedback will tell you how much you need to adjust your choice of line or putting speed.

The Effect of Green Speed

Before we move on to the next chapter, where you find out how to learn from your putt, there is one last factor to take into account: *friction*. The amount of friction determines whether the green is "slow" or "fast". On a sloped green, surface friction works against gravity, reducing its effect. (If there were no friction, the ball would never stop.)

The force of friction can also be represented by a vector, as shown in Figure 13: When two vectors oppose each other, they subtract, so the break in the putt (the net effect of gravity) is the result of subtracting the friction vector from the gravity vector.

How to Run an Experiment

To do the experiments described in this book, you need a ramp to roll the ball in a consistent direction, with consistent force.

For a rough version of the experiment, you can put two clubs side by side, hold them by the hosels, and brace your hand on your knee with the tips of the grips touching the ground. You now have a reasonably consistent ramp if you roll a ball along the grips. It's a short ramp, but the ball will run smoothly on to the green. (You might even find that a shoehorn works reasonably well.)

For a more accurate version of the experiment use a device such as the Pelz Tru-Roller (no longer made) or the Green Speed Reader (effective and convenient), or the high-end EyeLine Golf Sweet Roll Rail System. And be sure to have something handy to mark the target you're aiming at.

You might also consider taking along a yardstick to help be sure of your alignment, and a tape measure or cord to measure distances. (A cord works, because, for putting experiments, you're only concerned with maintaining the same distance from different angles. You don't need precise measurements.)

If you're gadget-happy (I am), you can take along an inclinometer like the BreakMaster Digital Reader or the EEZ-READ Green Reader to help you find the fall line. Or you can simply use your rolling device to roll the ball directly towards the hole, until it is moving directly to the center of the hole with no break in either direction. That's the fall line. Once you've found it, place a marker above or below the hole to keep you oriented.

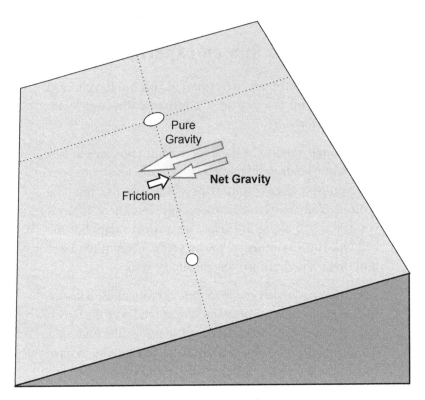

Figure 13: Gravity Minus Friction

Recall that *break* is the amount the ball travels downhill during a putt. With a slow green there is more friction, so the effect of gravity is weaker. As a result, there is less break. With a fast green there is less friction, and gravity's effect is stronger, so there is more break.

The important takeaway: A fast green with only a little slope will break as much as a slow green with a lot of slope.

A fast green with only a little slope breaks as much as a slow green with a lot of slope.

You generally don't have to worry about the friction component, though. Your only concern is the end result—the *net* gravitational force acting on the ball. As long as the greens are consistent, all you really have to be aware of is the amount of slope—and, in fact, that's all you *can* be aware of. Your eyes and your feet can tell how much slope there is. But they can't tell you how much surface friction there is.

The only way you can gauge green speed is when you've struck a ball (so you know how much force you applied) and you see how far it goes. It is relatively easy to compensate for differences in slope from hole to hole, because your mental computer can see and allow for it. But it is *extremely* difficult to compensate for differences in green speed.

To do that, you first have to know there *is* a difference, so you're watching for it. But even then, you have to know how *much* of a difference there is and how big of an adjustment to make—a practical impossibility.

That's why it's important for green speeds to be consistent from hole to hole. You now know why the tour players had so much trouble when the greens dried out at different speeds. On that day, each green had a different friction component, which made it impossible even for the best putters in the world to figure out where to aim and how forcefully to putt.

Learning from Your Putt

Where the ball finishes gives you precise information about your putt. Was it too fast, too slow, too high, or too low? In this chapter, we look at how the science of vector analysis discussed in the previous chapter helps you to determine exactly what went wrong with your putt—and how to use that feedback to make corrections.

The first step is to get that information into your internal computer. So hold your finish position, with your head tilted, and watch until the ball stops moving. Then, when you register the ball's final position, its path is automatically correlated with your putting stroke in an internal process that is below your conscious awareness, but which is highly effective nonetheless.

The next step is to *understand* what you're seeing, so you know what went wrong. After all, if you don't know what to correct, how can you possibly fix it? Look at every putt as an experiment that answers the two vital questions I introduced in the last chapter:

1. Did I have the right *read*?

2. Did I have the right *speed*?

The remainder of this chapter shows how the ball's final position gives precise answers to both of those questions. (How to do that is less well known than you'd think. Even professional TV commentators have been known to reach the wrong conclusion!)

Note:

The analysis is easiest to understand for a *sidehill* putt, where the ball is on the cross line that runs through the hole, perpendicular to the fall line. So, in this chapter, the ball is always in that position. In the next chapter, we'll deal with diagonal putts. The analysis will be similar, but the explanations will be shorter, since we will be building on the explanations given here.

Did You Have the Right Read?

After you putt, the first question to answer is whether or not you had the right read.

Vector analysis tells us that there is a perfect target point to aim at: where a ball traveling at the right amount of speed to overcome gravity will drop into the cup. That target point defines the line for the perfect putt. On that line, a ball struck with the right amount of force has a vertical component that is exactly enough to offset the force of gravity.

As shown in Figure 14, if you aim below that line, then the vertical component of the putt is insufficient to overcome gravity. Gravity wins, and the ball winds up "below the hole". That's easy to see when the ball is close to the hole. When the ball is farther away from the hole, "below the hole" means that the ball is below the cross line—the imaginary line that runs through the hole, perpendicular to the gravity axis.

As you can see in Figure 14, a point of aim that is below the ideal target means that the vertical component of the putt will be less than the gravitational force it is opposing. As we saw in the last chapter, opposing vectors subtract from one another, so the putt winds up below the cross line—the exact distance below is equal to the difference between the vertical component and the gravitational force. Whether the putt is short or long, it winds up on the *finish line* below the hole.

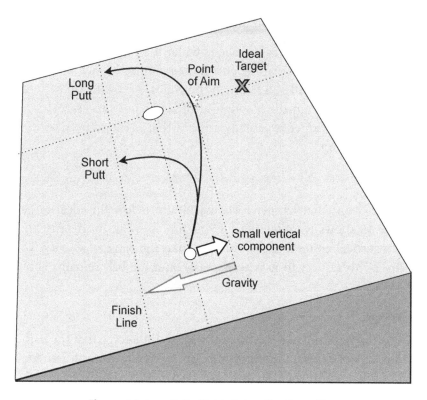

Figure 14: Low Putts Finish Below the Cross Line

There is some leeway, of course. A putt that is short of the perfect line can still make it into the hole, if it carries enough speed. It would be like a flat basketball shot, as opposed to one that arcs smoothly to the hoop. But while a "flat" putt can work, it only works up to a point. If it is too flat and too fast, it can pop right over the hole. So there is a range in which a less than perfect putt still works, but in general, a putt that is below the ideal line winds up "below the hole"—in other words, below the cross line.

The Ideal Target

We can think of the ideal target as a single point (the "aim point", in some systems) such that a putt aimed at it with perfect force will land precisely in the middle of the cup.

But in reality, since the cup is wider than the ball, there is margin for error. A putt aimed a little higher or a little lower will still fall in at the edges, so it will still be "perfect", from the standpoint of achieving success. So the ideal target is actually an area that is the same size as the cup.

We've seen what happens when you aim below the ideal target. Figure 15 shows what happens if you aim above it. In this case, the putt's vertical component is stronger than the force of gravity. You "win" (with respect to gravity, at least), and the ball remains above the hole.

Note:

It is theoretically possible to putt with so little force that the ball doesn't even *reach* the finish line. But generally your awareness of the slope and your desire to get the ball to the hole causes you to putt with enough force to produce a useful result.

Again, the ball's position relative to the hole is easiest to see when the ball is near the hole. The farther away it gets, the more helpful it is to visualize the cross line, to see where the ball is in relation to that line.

The cross line, then, is the *midpoint* between a putt that is aimed too low and one that is aimed too high. This means if the ball stops anywhere on the cross line, you know you chose the right line. Your speed may have been off, but you definitely had the right read.

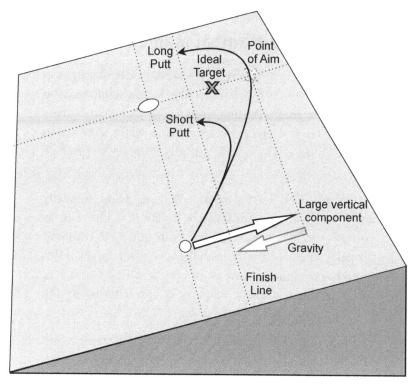

Figure 15: High Putts Finish Above the Cross Line

In other words, for a sidehill putt, *the cross line is the READ line.* And that line is also the *sight line.*

**For a sidehill putt,
the cross line is the READ line.
That line is also the sight line.**

The cross line can be difficult to see when you're far above the hole, or far below it. It's easiest to see when you have a sidehill putt from directly on the cross line. So it makes sense to practice breaking putts from that vantage point. That way, the cross line is also your sight line to the hole. It is then easy to see where the ball finishes in relation to the cross line.

The Magical Moment

If you're like most, you've never seen a sidehill putt stop *above* the hole. That's where feedback comes into play on the practice green. Putting from a spot that is 90 degrees from the fall line gives you a sight line that is identical to the cross line—which makes it a great place to practice from.

When you first start working on your putts, virtually every ball will stop somewhere below that line. But as you learn to take feedback from your putts—to read and properly evaluate them—you'll move your target point higher and higher up the slope. Eventually, a wonderful thing happens: You reach a point of aim from where the ball comes to rest *above* the hole.

The first time that happens, it is a truly magical moment. You have found out that it is *possible* to aim high enough to have the ball stop above the hole—even on a steep slope. Because most amateurs never learn how far above the hole they actually have to aim, a miss on the low side is called an "amateur miss", while a miss on the high side is a "professional miss". The change from "amateur" to "professional" is learning that you *can* stop the ball above the hole—and finding out just how *far* above the hole you have to aim for that to happen.

The AimPoint system has some charts showing that, on a steep, fast green, the target could be as far as *17 feet* above the hole, depending on your distance from the cup. That was a revelation for me, when I took their class. You can have your own epiphany in that regard, by spending a little time on the fastest, steepest practice green you can find.

Exactly How Far Off Were You?

From the standpoint of taking feedback from the putt, it is the *distance* below the cross line that is significant. In the next two diagrams, that difference is identified by "d", the standard mathematical symbol for the Greek letter δ, which is pronounced *delta* and often used in math to represent difference.

As shown in Figure 16, the delta (distance) the ball stops below the cross line is *identical* to the delta between the actual target and the ideal target (on a green with a constant slope). So the ball's finishing position tells you *exactly* how much your read was off.

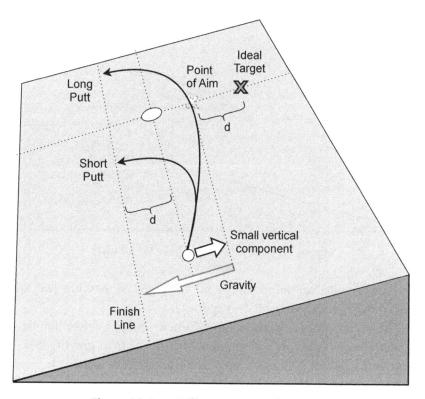

Figure 16: Exact Difference Below Ideal Target

Similarly, Figure 17 shows the delta for a ball that was aimed high. Once again, the delta between the ideal target and the point of aim is identical to the distance the ball finishes above the hole. Again, assuming that the slope is constant, the ball's finishing position tells you *exactly* how far your read was off.

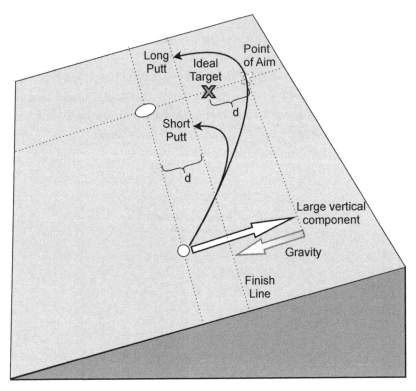

Figure 17: Exact Difference Above Ideal Target

These results can be proven by the magic of vectors, but you can also prove them to yourself, by experiment.

The vector proof is pretty simple: When you aim above the ideal target, the putt's vertical component is stronger than gravity. When you aim below it, the putt's vertical component is weaker. In each case, the vertical component subtracts from gravity (or vice versa), and what's left is the amount of force acting on the ball in the vertical direction. Physics says that the ball *has* to finish above or below its starting point on the cross line, at a point determined by the magnitude of that vector.

To prove it by experiment, all you need is a constant slope, and a ramp you can use to roll a ball at a fixed speed in a fixed direction. First, find the direction and position on the ramp that rolls a breaking ball into the hole. Mark that point on the fall line, then aim at a higher or lower point. When the ball stops, measure its height above or below the hole and compare it with the difference between the point of aim and ideal target.

When you're playing, knowing how far you were off is pretty helpful. But that information is *especially* helpful on the practice green, because it tells you how much to adjust your subsequent putts. That feedback lets you rapidly dial in the right read, which works wonders to improve your green reading skills.

3-Ball Practice
(The "Rule of Three")

It's possible to become very, very good in the practice area, and still be unable to perform on the course. The reason: When you repeat the same motion 20 or 30 times, you can groove it in nicely. But then, when you go to the course, you get exactly *one* swing from a particular lie, with a particular club. And you get exactly *one* putt from a given distance, on a given slope.

Your practices need to simulate those conditions—changing locations on the putting green (or changing clubs at the range), setting up your shot, and then taking your stroke. When you do that, you're practicing the same routine you'll be using when you play—mentally sizing up the situation, deciding on a course of action, and then taking a stroke.

But you *also* need to get feedback from your strokes, and make adjustments. It is seriously difficult to improve, unless you do. And the ability to get feedback and adjust requires repetition of a single movement.

(continued on next page)

•••

To resolve the dilemma, I advocate putting 3 balls from a single location in practice, before moving on. The first putt gives you information. The second lets you refine it. By the third, you will (ideally) be dialed in. (At least, your *read* will be dialed in. It will still take time to dial in your stroke.) Moving to a new location at that point better simulates game conditions, where no 2 strokes are ever the same.

Putting 3 balls at a time, therefore, strikes a balance between improving your read, perfecting your stroke, and continually changing conditions, which helps you develop skills you can take to the course. I use that same principle at the driving range, changing clubs every 3 swings or so, if things are going well. If things aren't going well with a particular club, I'll spend more time with it. But if I've had 3 good swings, I'm done with that club for the moment. I may well come back to it as I move up and down the clubs in my bag, and do different-size swings with them. But as a general guideline, I use "the rule of three"—and when I'm taking 3 swings with every club, I know that I'm "on", for that day, at least.

Did You Have the Right Speed?

The next question is whether or not you had the right speed. You've already seen that if you putt the ball towards the hole with perfect speed to reach it, and the green is sloped, the ball comes to rest below the hole, directly on the fall line. And we know that there is an ideal "dead drop" target—where a ball aimed at that point, struck with perfect pace, will drop into the hole.

So that's 2 putts that we know end up on the fall line, if the speed is right. For a putt on any other line, we can do the same kind of analysis that we did in the previous section—only this time, we examine the horizontal component of the putt vector.

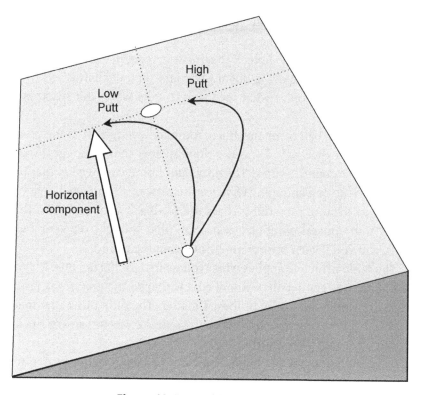

Figure 18: Putts with Perfect Speed

Whether you putt high or low, if the horizontal component is enough to reach the fall line, then the speed was perfect (as you can see in Figure 18). After all, if the line you putted on had been right, the ball would have dropped into the hole. It's hard to get any better than that.

The same kind of analysis we did in the last section tells us that if you putt harder than that, the horizontal component takes the ball past the fall line. Putt easier, and the ball stays short of the fall line. So if the ball comes to rest on the fall line, you know you had the right speed for the line you chose. In other words, *the fall line is the SPEED line.*

The fall line is the SPEED line.

For every breaking putt you make, you need to putt with just enough force to reach the fall line. If you do, and the line was right, the ball winds up in the hole. If the line wasn't right, the ball winds up above the hole, or below it, but always right on the fall line.

The next question is what feedback to take when the speed isn't perfect.

Let's say, the ball came up short. You may wonder, "Was the green slower than expected?", "Was the slope steeper than I thought?" The answer is, *it doesn't matter!* The only take-home you need is that the putt wasn't strong enough. *Whatever* the reason, all you need to know is to putt it more forcefully. That's the feedback you take from that shot. Your mental computer will apply that thought on your next putt, and you'll keep improving throughout the round.

The same principle applies when you overshoot the fall line. Maybe the slope was gentler than it looked. Or maybe the green was faster than you thought. Again, it doesn't matter. The only thing that matters is that on this green, on this day, the stroke was too strong. It's all about matching your effort to the conditions.

So don't automatically blame yourself for being a poor putter, for being weak, or over-hitting, or for any other of 10 dozen reasons for getting down on yourself. Forget all that! Simply take the feedback from the shot at hand—because the fact of the matter is that no one can see the speed of the green. The best you can do is to figure it out over time, from experience.

The Finishing Quadrants

Depending on where the ball stops, then, you can tell if you had the wrong speed, the wrong line, or both. And you can tell by *how much* each of those variables was off.

In summary, for a sidehill putt:

- The fall line is the SPEED line, and the cross line/sight line is the READ line.
- If the ball stops on the cross line, you had the right read, but not the right speed.
- If it stops above the cross line, the line was high. If it stops below the cross line, the line was low.
- If the ball stops on the fall line (which means that at the last second it was moving downhill directly towards the hole or directly away from it), then you had the right speed, but not the right read.
- If the ball stops short of the fall line, it was struck too softly. If it stops beyond the fall line, it was struck too hard.

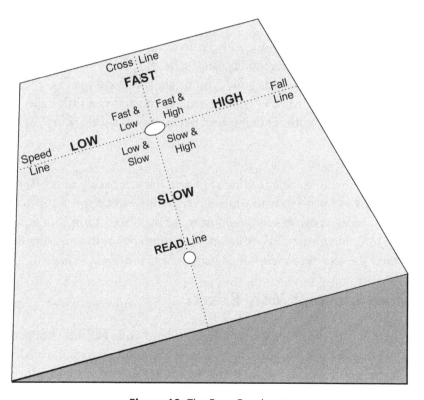

Figure 19: The Four Quadrants

Figure 19 shows the four quadrants created by those observations:

- If the ball stops short of the fall line and above the cross line, it was too slow and aimed too high.

- If it stops beyond the fall line and above the cross line, it was too fast and aimed too high.

- If it stops short of the fall line and below the cross line, it was too slow and aimed too low.

- If it stops beyond the fall line and below the cross line, it was too fast and aimed too low.

You can use those principles to *evaluate your putt*. In fact, you can use them to evaluate every putt you see—on TV and the ones your playing partners make.

Note:

In front of the television, you can freely speak your mind, but, in the interest of congeniality, only state the positives with your partners. If the line was good, you might say "good read". If the speed was right, maybe "good speed". At most, give a little valuable feedback, without being negative, such as "a little short", or "a bit high".

But the most important thing is to give the feedback you get from *your* putts to *yourself*. Say to yourself, "right line, wrong speed", or "too low", or whatever works for you. Just make the observation. You don't have to do anything else. Your internal computer will work silently behind the scenes to make an adjustment for your next stroke.

More Speed or More Break?

When you tilt your head and take in where your ball has stopped (if it's not in the hole), use the finishing quadrant system and make a mental note of the required correction. (Knowing what to adjust helps your mental computer a lot.)

If you follow that policy religiously, you're going to get better and better from hole to hole, and from game to game. You can even practice while watching the players on TV. It's a lot harder to see the fall line accurately, but you can get a general sense of what's going to happen. Most importantly, you can practice the learning part of the process, where you find the fall line from the last inch of travel, and then determine whether the speed or the line was off.

The feedback step is crucial because good putting isn't just about making the putt—it is also about managing your misses. Ideally, you want the ball to be so close to the hole that the second putt is a stress-free tap-in.

For example, suppose you think you need more speed, when you *really* should be correcting the line to allow more break. Putting faster can work in that case—but only up to a point. There is an upper limit. Too much speed and your ball can roll over the hole. More importantly, if it's your first putt the goal is to make sure that if you do miss, the next one is a virtual certainty.

As I've said, we amateurs tend to miss on the low side, because we don't allow enough break. Nevertheless, if your speed is perfect, that low-side miss will be a direct uphill putt—the easiest kind of putt to make from any reasonable distance. So getting the speed right is extremely important. Taking the wrong message from your putts can cause you to increase your putting speed even when, in reality, the speed was perfect.

Unless you *know* that your speed was right, you may well be tempted to try putting harder—especially if someone tells you that you should. But what happens if you increase your speed? At times, it will work. But when you miss, you miss with a much greater margin of error than if you had adjusted your line—and the come-backer will be quite a bit harder.

The quadrant system I've shown you makes it possible to *know* when you have the right read, and when you have the right speed. Without it, it would be easy to make the mistake of thinking you should be putting harder.

You would not be alone in making that kind of mistake, either. Even professional commentators do it, as related in the sidebar.

Even Announcers Can Get it Wrong

The greens are such a mystery that even professional golfers who became announcers have been known to get it wrong. For example, the ball might land below the hole, precisely on the fall line, (which indicates the speed was perfect), and at times you'll hear the commentator say "He didn't hit it hard enough". It happens more often than you might think.

He didn't hit it hard enough? Sure, it's *possible* to hit the ball hard enough to take out a foot of break. And if you make it, fine. But if you miss—by even a little bit—on the kind of fast green the pros play on, the ball winds up way beyond the hole!

At the 2016 WGC-Cadillac Championship at Doral, Australian Adam Scott missed an 18-footer for eagle on the 8th green. That putt was a thing of *beauty*. The ball went above the hole about a foot and a half and then, as it slowed, it arced gracefully, coming to rest about a foot and a half directly behind the cup, right on the sight line.

Clearly, the read was *perfect*. Had the speed been right, he would have holed it. The commentator's remark? "It's crazy that he would misread the putt by that much. That's something he really needs to work on. He missed that putt by a foot and a half!"

Well, yes. The ball was a foot and a half high as it went by the hole. But it only went *by* because it was too fast. The ball *had to be that high*. On that line, gravity pulled the ball to level of the hole as it slowed down, just before coming to a stop on the sight line, behind the hole. The ball's finishing position said so. There was no problem with

• • •

his read, but if he listened to the (otherwise very expert and highly informative) advice from the commentator, he could wind up making the wrong corrections entirely. Worse, everyone who listened to that broadcast got the wrong message!

(To be fair, the announcer no doubt meant that Scott should have chosen the right line *and* putted with the right speed. But what he *said* in the heat of the moment was "misread", which was unfortunately misleading for those listening.)

The take-home: When the ball goes too low, but it finishes on the fall line, you need to correct your line—*not* your speed. If your line is off, you may have misread the slope, or maybe the green was faster than expected. Which was it? *It doesn't matter.* In either case, you need to allow more break than you thought.

Over time, as you get feedback on putt after putt, you'll tend to become a master of allowing the right amount of break for normal green speeds. And when you're on a course where the greens are consistently faster or slower than you're used to, you'll automatically adjust as you take feedback from each putt you make.

Next, we look at how these scientific principles of green reading and feedback can help you deal with the other pesky, awkward problems … uh, I mean, *opportunities* … that make up the game of golf.

Vertical and Diagonal Putts

The system you've been learning in this book establishes an analytic framework for understanding the results of a putt. What you've learned so far works very well when the ball is sitting on the cross line, perpendicular to the fall line. In that situation, your sight line from the ball to the hole is identical to the cross line. That makes it easy to see and understand the results of each putt.

But what happens when the ball is not on the cross line? In this chapter, we'll see what vector analysis can tell us about "vertical" and "diagonal" putts. We'll start with vertical putts from directly above or below the hole.

Straight Uphill and Downhill

When the ball is sitting on the fall line and you're putting straight uphill or downhill, the analysis is pretty easy. We don't even need vectors. But it is instructive to examine that situation, nonetheless.

Our first observation is that the line to the hole (the sight line) is now the READ line, as shown in Figure 20. If you putt the ball directly towards the hole from that position, and it goes to the left or right, then it must have been that the ball wasn't on the fall line—which means that your read was off. (We are assuming your putt goes down the line you aimed.)

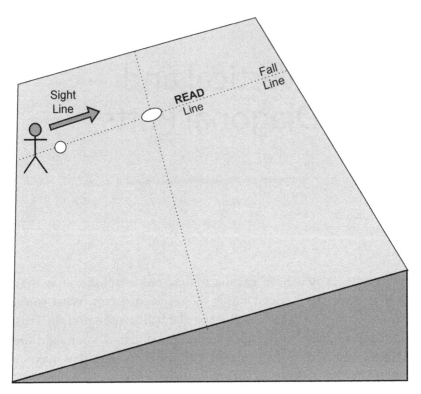

Figure 20: Vertical Putt. Sight Line = READ Line

In this case, the line to the hole is the fall line, as well. Earlier we observed that the sight (or cross) line is the READ line for a sidehill putt. And for this putt, we see that the read line is again the sight line (as well as the fall line). What the two types of putts have in common is the sight line. (The logical next question is, will this principle work for diagonal putts, as well? In the next section, we see it does.)

Okay, we know that the line to the hole (the sight line) is the fall line. And we know the sight line is the READ line. The only thing left is to find that SPEED line, which is also pretty easy.

In this situation, the cross line is the speed line, as shown in Figure 21. If the ball doesn't get to the hole, it falls short. If it gets there with almost any speed, it probably drops. If you leave it short, the distance between the ball's finishing position and the hole tells you exactly how much farther the ball needed to travel to make the putt. (Duh. It's obvious. I know. But we're setting up the background we need to dissect the diagonal putts. That's next.)

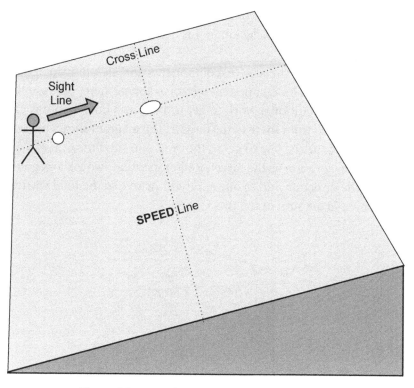

Figure 21: Vertical Putt. Cross Line = SPEED Line

Uphill Diagonal

At this point, we've dealt with perfectly perpendicular horizontal putts and vertical putts. Now it's time to address everything in between—the diagonal putts. First, we'll see what happens when the line is right but the speed is off, and in the next section, what happens when the read is off.

Note:

In all of these analyses, we are assuming that the force of gravity is constant. In other words, once the ball starts moving, a given amount of gravity acceleration operates on the ball as soon as the friction that was holding the ball in place is broken. In reality, there is probably a difference between short putts and long ones. But I'm choosing to ignore that complication in the interests of reaching some sort of useful conclusion in this decade.

Figure 22 shows the vector components for an uphill diagonal putt. The anti-gravity component-vector is longer here, because the putt has to do additional work to get to the cross line, before it can proceed upward from there to the target. (The diagram shows the two vertical components, one to get to the cross line, and the other to get to the same elevation as the target. Remember that two vectors going in the same direction add to one another linearly, so the total vertical component is the sum of the two.)

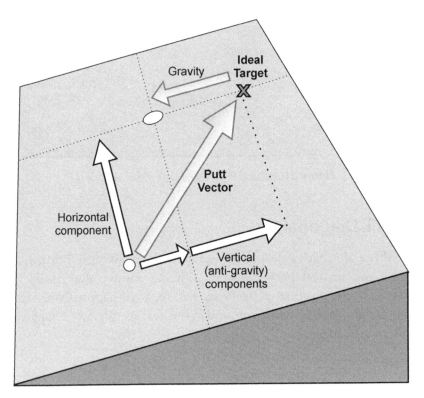

Figure 22: Diagonal Putt Vector Components

With perfect velocity, the ball would be coming to a stop just as it reaches the fall line. On a sloped green, that velocity means that the force of gravity has been completely counteracted on the vertical (gravity) axis, with just enough vertical force to get the ball up to the level of the hole, and just enough horizontal velocity to get the ball over to it. Result: One sunk putt. (Once again, the ball's actual path will be curved, but the vector analysis shows where the forces are directed.)

First, let's see what happens if you have the right line, but the wrong speed.

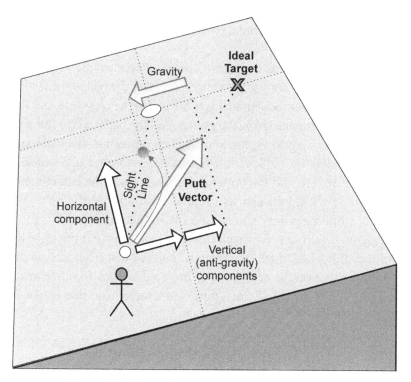

Figure 23: Diagonal Putt, Right Read, Wrong Speed

The result is shown in Figure 23. The putt was on the perfect line, but was too slow. The force vector goes past the cross line, but is not sufficient to fully counteract the effects of gravity. As a result, the ball finishes below the hole.

Since the ball finishes below the hole, you could easily conclude that the line you chose was wrong, when it was actually your speed that was off. How can you tell? Because if you have the right line, the ball *stops on your sight line* to the hole—every time.

If you have the right read, the ball stops on the sight line—every time.

This is a principle you can prove to yourself, by experiment. Use a ramp (as we've seen before), for consistent direction and velocity, and a hole on a consistent slope. Once you find the position and speed that puts the ball into the hole, try slower and faster speeds. You'll see the results for yourself.

First, mentally extend the putt vector so it reaches the ideal target. With that speed, the horizontal component takes the ball to the fall line, while the vertical component first gets the ball to the cross line, and then overcomes the remaining force of gravity, and the ball lands in the hole.

Now reduce the putt vector to near zero. Of course, the ball barely moves from its original location. Then keep adding degrees of force between near zero and the target point. Each time, the ball comes to a stop somewhere between its original location and the hole. That series of stopping points is none other than the sight line.

The conclusion to reach from this experiment is that the sight line is *always* the READ line, whether the ball is on the fall line, is perpendicular to it on the cross line, or is on a diagonal. In other words, the sight line is the READ line, pure and simple. And that is true for all putts. Always.

The sight line is the READ line.
For all putts. Always!

Downhill "Slider"

Now that we know where the READ line is, let's find the SPEED line. That's easiest to do with a diagonal downhill putt, as shown in Figure 24.

That kind of putt is sometimes called a *slider*, because the ball appears to break more than it does for any other putt. (That is, however, an illusion, which we'll discuss more in the chapter on "Getting a Break", under the heading One Target to Rule Them All.)

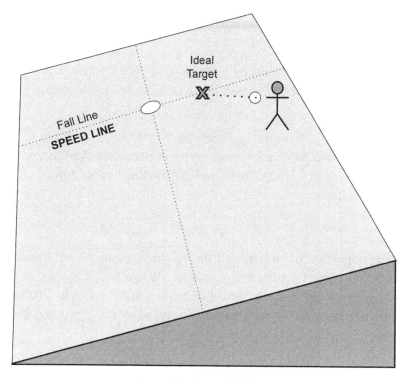

Figure 24: Downhill Slider

The first constant is that the fall line is still the SPEED line. That principle is pretty easy to understand. If the ball's last inch of travel is directly towards the hole when it comes to a stop, you had the right speed for the line you choose—it was just the wrong line.

A couple of observations: First, it is theoretically possible for a strong putt to bounce over the cup, like Evel Knievel jumping over a canyon. (A power putter might do that, once in a while. A die at the hole putter never will.) Second, even if you had the wrong "fall line" in mind when you aimed, the direction the ball is traveling in the last inch before it stops tells you the actual fall line.

Cross Line as Speed Line

If the ball doesn't make it to the cross line, then clearly it was not carrying enough speed to make it to the hole. So in that sense, the cross line is a speed line, too—especially on a more vertical putt.

So when you're putting from near the fall line, feel free to register the ball's finishing position with respect to the cross line.

However, once you've committed to a putt, the more important feedback is how well you putted *on that line*. That is the feedback that will pay the largest future dividends.

The important point here is if the ball finishes on the fall line, *the speed was perfect for the line you chose.* When that happens, don't beat yourself up because you didn't hit it hard enough. Instead, recognize that your speed was terrific and work on improving your read.

**If the ball finishes on the fall line,
the speed was perfect for the line you chose.**

The bottom line, then, is that the fall line is *always* the SPEED line, whether the ball is on the fall line, is perpendicular to it on the cross line, or is on a diagonal. In other words, the fall line is the SPEED line. For every putt. Always.

**The fall line is the SPEED line.
For every putt. Always!**

The second constant is that the sight line is still the READ line, as shown in Figure 25. If your ball finishes on the sight line, your line was perfect, even if the speed was off. You can run an experiment to see that result for yourself, as well.

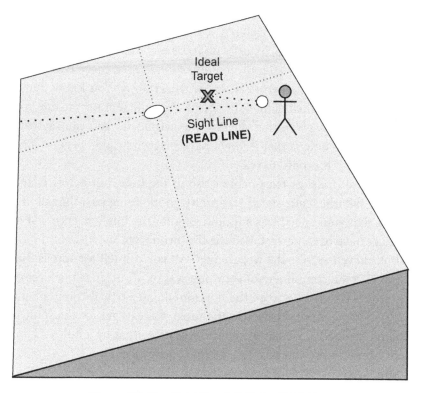

Figure 25: The Sight Line Is Still the READ Line

How Far Off Was Your Speed?

For a downhill putt, there are two ways to answer the question, as noted earlier.

The best answer is in relation to the fall line. The distance between the ball and your fall line tells you exactly how far off your speed was for the line you chose.

The other answer is in relation to the cross line. If the ball makes it to the cross line, and it's close to the hole, then the speed was *probably* sufficient to sink the putt. But the further away the ball is from the hole, the more reliable the fall line becomes, as a guide for speed.

For example, if the ball stops on the cross line well short of the hole, then no, it likely did not have enough speed to get to the hole. If it stops on the cross line well past the hole, then it probably had too much speed—but again, it's difficult to be certain.

For an uphill diagonal putt, that question is even more tricky, and there is not too much you can say with certainty. You know that if the ball stops on the fall line, the speed was sufficient for the line you chose. However, given that the line was wrong, all you can say with respect to the hole is that it *might* have been the right speed to sink the putt—but it is hard to tell.

If the ball finishes reasonably close to the hole, but below it and *past* the fall line, your speed was pretty good. Being past the fall line means that your speed was a little strong for the line you chose—but it might have been perfect, had the line been right.

But I have to stress the word *might*. All you can tell for sure is that the horizontal component of your putt was off—but since the force of the putt is divided between the horizontal and vertical components, it's hard to be more precise. So the most you can get for that putt is general feedback that says the speed was off (either by a little or a lot depending on how far past the fall line you are).

Similarly, if the ball finishes close to the hole and above it, then your speed and read were also pretty good. Again, it's hard to be more precise.

In other words, the only *consistent* way to judge speed is relative to the line you chose. And the best way to do that is in relation to the fall line.

Golf is a game of the imperfect, so take the feedback you can get, and use it to improve your next putt.

How Far Off Was Your Read?

Let's start by assuming that whatever line you chose, you hit it with perfect speed—the speed that carries the ball to the fall line. With that speed, the ball always finishes on the fall line. But also assuming you have missed the hole, the question is, how far off was your read?

As shown in Figure 26, with perfect speed, the distance the ball finishes below the cross line is exactly equal to the distance your read was off from the ideal target. Vector analysis tells us that the result cannot turn out any other way. (This, too, is an experiment you can try for yourself.)

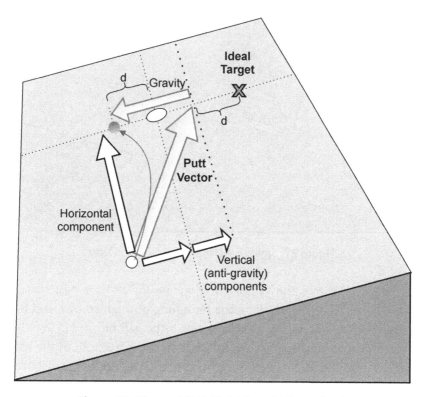

Figure 26: Diagonal Putt, Right Speed, Wrong Read

The hole is at the intersection of *three* lines—the fall line, the cross line, and the sight line. When the speed isn't perfect, but your line (the target line) is, we know that the ball finishes on the sight line. So, conversely, where the ball finishes in relation to the sight line tells you exactly how far off you were from the perfect read, as shown in Figure 27.

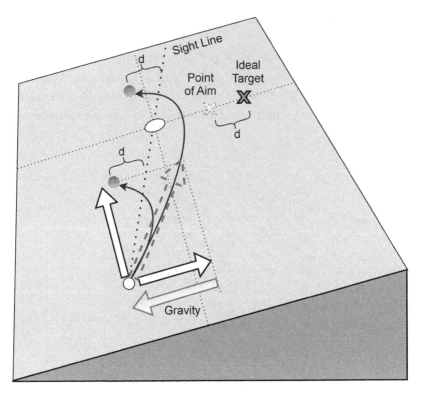

Figure 27: Sight Line Delta = Ideal Target Delta

Figure 27 shows the vector components for a short putt that is aimed low. Things work the same for a long putt aimed low, and for putts that are aimed high. In each case, if the ball finishes below the sight line, your target was lower than it should have been. If the ball finishes above that line, your target was high. And again, the distance between the sight line and the ball's finishing position shows exactly how far your aim was off.

Fine Tuning

N ow that you have the basics in place, this chapter adds a few refinements.

You're Putting to a Large Target Area!

You can begin to take the pressure off your putting by remembering the following key points:

- As you take feedback from putt after putt, your ability to find the right point of aim will improve from green to green, and round to round.

- Your ability to putt to that spot with the right amount of force will also improve from green to green, and round to round.

- With your putting and green-reading skills, your first putt *only needs to be within a few feet* of the ideal target.

If you're 5 or 6 feet away, you'd like to finish within a foot or so of the hole. From 10 to 15 feet, you'd like to be within 2 feet. But from any kind of distance, getting within 3 feet of the hole is just fine.

Closer in is better, of course. but anywhere within a reasonable radius is fine. For a long putt, that's 3 feet, *anywhere around the hole*, which means your putt only needs to be *within 3 feet of the ideal target*, as shown in Figure 28.

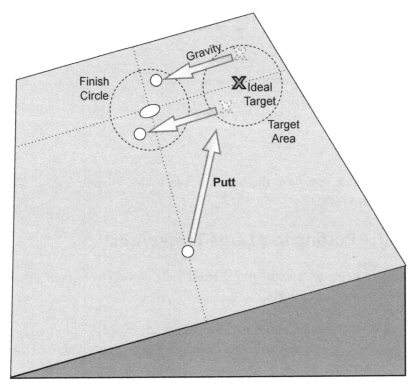

Figure 28: Target Area Maps to Finish Area

The point of Figure 28 is that the target area maps directly to the finishing area! The reason: The effect of gravity is constant for a given slope and green speed. If a ball is played to the ideal target spot, it lands in the pocket. If the ball is high or low, fast or slow, the exact same gravity vector is working on it. Whether your aim is slightly off or your putting is slightly off, any ball that is played to within a few feet of the ideal target winds up that same distance from the hole.

In other words, from any kind of distance, your target circle is 6 *feet* in diameter.

**From any kind of distance,
your target circle is 6 feet across.**

The good news is that your read doesn't have to be perfect! It just needs to be within a few feet of the ideal target. And your putt doesn't have to be perfect, either. As long as you can putt somewhere near the target you selected, and your target is somewhere near the ideal, you're in *great* shape. The better your read, the more leeway you have in your putt. And the better your putt, the more leeway you have in your read.

Pressure? What pressure? From any kind of distance, 2 putts will be required most of the time! Even the pros miss 50% of their putts from 6 feet, and the percentage drops rapidly at longer distances.

Sure, give the ball the best possible chance to drop. But if your target is anywhere in that huge circle, you're fine. Zero pressure! With your new putt-reading skills, 3-footers are practically a "gimme", and even 4- and 5-footers are makeable with the information you gain from your first putt—especially as your speed improves and you leave more putts on the fall line.

As your initial putt dies, it tells you where the fall line really is, regardless of where you originally thought it was. With that information, and with the green-reading and putting skills you develop over time, virtually every 3-footer is makeable.

The pros make 90% of the 3-footers they face. With what you're learning, you will too! So if you are anywhere within 3 feet of the ideal target, you are virtually guaranteed a 2-putt.

Learn the Right Lesson (Practice Quiz)

Here's a quiz for you: Figure 29 shows four different trajectories and finishing positions. In each case, the ball starts on the cross line to the left (so the sight line and cross line are the same, which makes analysis easier), and finishes in the lower right quadrant.

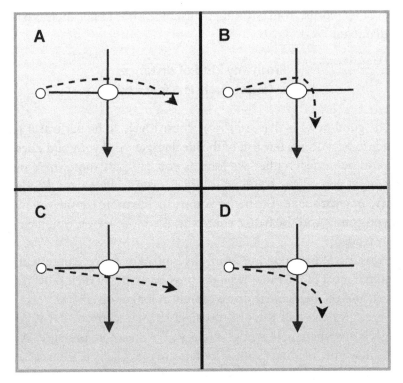

Figure 29: Four Different Finishing Positions

Examine each diagram, and see what you think happened. What were the adjustments that should have been made? Then compare your conclusions with the ones below.

A. Ball Crosses Above, Goes Long
The break was shallow. The ball came close, but went long. We can conclude the read was decent and, with better speed, it would have dropped. Speed needs slowing considerably. With this flat a slope, there is no way that amount of speed could ever be right.

B. Ball Crosses Above, Goes Low
There was obviously a lot of break in this putt, for the ball to go so low after missing the hole. Speed was okay, and might have been right for a better (higher) line, but it was really the

read that was off. To hole it, there would need to be a significant adjustment to the line.

C. Ball Crosses Below, Goes Long

Again, a shallow slope. Read was a tad low, so the ball never had a chance. But, as with example A, speed was the big factor and needs adjusting the most.

D. Ball Crosses Below, Goes Low

Again, the ball never had a chance, because the read was so far off. Speed was good for the line chosen, but especially on this slope, with this green speed, the read needs a lot of adjustment.

Maximum and Minimum Adjustments

Examples 29-C and 29-D in the previous section are particularly instructive.

We know that when a putt finishes on the fall line, the distance from the ball to the hole tells us the exact amount that the read was off (assuming a constant slope). But when a putt goes long, gravity acts on it longer, so the ball finishes lower than it would have had it finished on the fall line. (Similarly, it finishes higher than it would have if it comes to rest short of the fall line.)

In example D, the ball stops well below the cross line. The ideal adjustment to the read will use that distance, so the ball trickles into the hole. But that is the *maximum* adjustment. With the right speed, smaller adjustments will work, too.

In examples C and D, the point where the ball crosses the fall line gives you the *minimum* adjustment you need to make to be successful, while the ball's finishing position gives you the *maximum* adjustment. With the minimum adjustment, and the right speed, you can still hole the ball. With the maximum adjustment, the ball should just trickle into the slope if you get it to the fall line—even on a very steep slope.

So anywhere between the minimum adjustment and the maximum adjustment to the read will work, as long as the speed is right for that line.

I'm a big fan of dying the ball at the hole, so I recommend trying to make the maximum adjustment—especially when practicing. It is instructive to see just how far above a hole you have to aim to get the ball close on a steep slope or fast green.

Similarly, if the ball stops short of the fall line, the read was off by the distance from the cross line, plus a bit. (To figure out how much, you have to imagine the ball traveling fast enough to reach the fall line, and determine where it probably would have stopped, had it gotten there.)

When line and speed are both off, determining exactly how much to adjust on each dimension becomes a matter of *feel*. But once you can understand and evaluate the results of every putt you observe, you'll find that your "feel" improves tremendously—and much more rapidly than you may have thought possible.

Making the *Right* Adjustment

We know that the fall line crossing gives you the minimum adjustment for a low putt, but things are a bit more complex for a ball that crosses the fall line above the hole, as in examples 29-A and 29-B. After all, if the ball crosses high, then the read must have been high, right?

Well, no. It's true that had the line been lower, the arc of the ball would have intersected the hole. BUT… and this is a big but … if you miss, your next putt is that much more horrible.

So while you *could* choose to putt lower, it would be a mistake to do so—especially in example B, where a steep slope has the ball going far below the hole when you miss. Adding extra distance to that equation is a recipe for a 4-putt, never mind a 3-putt.

The moral then, is that when a ball goes low and ends low, the fall line crossing gives you useful information. But when the ball goes high (above the hole), and *still* ends low, the ball's finishing position is the best indicator, not the fall line crossing.

In Case of Doubt, Adjust Your Speed

The major lesson to be learned from the preceding examples is that whichever dimension is off the most is the one that is most in need of adjustment. And making those adjustments in practice is the best way to improve your reads and speeds on the course.

I will only add that if both are off in equal measure, proper speed gives you the best possible follow-up putt, as you've seen. You can live with a read that's a little off. It's hard to get it perfect, since the speed and slope of every green is slightly different. But *distance* is something that is more under your control.

Of course, green speed has a lot to do with how far the ball travels, but you've been learning about green speed with every putt you make—so your goal should be perfect speed for every putt.

A Case of Changing Speed

I was playing in a Northern California Golf Association (NCGA) teacher's pro-am, where local teachers were paired with local amateurs, giving amateurs a great learning opportunity while allowing the teachers to compare themselves to other teachers, to see who got the most out of their protégés.

As an amateur, I was paired with Bill Troyanoski, from Half Moon Bay. The one part of my game that was really good was on the greens, and by the end of the round, my speed was pretty well "dialed in".

The greens had been aerated a few weeks earlier, to improve grass growth. So they were slower than normal, due to the rivulets of sand filling the small trenches that were running through the greens. But they weren't terribly slow, and they were consistent, so I was doing well.

(continued on next page)

• • •

Then we got to the last green. We had started on the 17th hole, as our place in the "shotgun" start, and had now worked our way back around to the 16th. That hole was just outside the maintenance shed, which didn't register one way or another at the time—until I made my putt.

To my surprise, the putt *raced* past the hole, easily going twice as far past as any other putt I had made. What the heck happened? I wondered. Then I noticed that the grass on that particular green had almost completely filled in the sandy areas.

Since that green was right outside the maintenance shed, that must have been the first green they worked on. Then they went to the 17th, and so on. Because the 16th had been done first, that green was almost completely healed. So it was close to normal speed. The 17th was slightly slower. The 18th was slightly slower than that, and so on.

Throughout the round, I had been playing on greens that were progressively slower, because they had been aerated more recently. I had unconsciously been making the adjustment each time, and was never very far off the right pace, until we jumped from the recently aerated 15th to the almost-completely-healed 16th.

My putt was so much faster on that green that I wondered what on earth had happened. That was when I looked at the green closely, and noticed that the sandy trenches I had become used to were almost totally gone. I had been ambushed!

When the Ball Goes in the Cup

We've had a lot to say about what you can learn when the ball misses the cup, but there are things to be learned when it goes in, as well. If you're paying really close attention, you can gain useful information that lets you make "micro-adjustments" to your green-reading and putting skills.

If the ball goes in too fast, there isn't much to be learned. In that case, putting force is still dominating the equation, and the lessons to be learned are few. But if the ball goes in slowly, or better yet trickles in, there is still information to be gained.

If someone else is putting, the last inch or two of travel before the ball goes into the cup gives you a clue as to the fall line. It's not as accurate as a ball that comes to rest, but it's helpful.

When you're putting, you want to observe where the ball enters the cup, in relation to the fall line.

Once you know the direction of the fall line, imagine it bisecting the cup, straight down the middle. If the ball enters the cup on that line, you had perfect pace for the line you chose, and a perfect read for that pace. In other words, you landed dead center.

If the ball enters the cup beyond that line, you were a little fast. Short of it, and the pace was a tad slow, for that line.

The important thing is that you made the putt. The information you get amounts to fine-tuning—*very* fine tuning. It's not like you get a lot of information, but the premise of this book is that feedback is a vital element of the putt, so take everything you can get!

The Ideal Entry Point

From directly above the hole, the possible entry points are on the half of the cup you can see, as shown in Figure 30-A. The ball can topple in from either side, or it can go directly into the middle.

The ideal entry point is the middle of the cup for those putts. That point removes the possibility of a lip-out, and gives you maximum protection against a minor bump in the green. (As Dave Pelz points out in his Putting Bible, the slight depressions made by people's feet create a "lumpy donut" of bumps and dips around the hole, up to 6 feet out. That's certainly true for greens of average softness, which is part of the reason why professionals prefer hard, fast greens—they're more consistent, and it doesn't take a power putt to drive the ball past surface irregularities.)

From directly perpendicular to the fall line, on the cross line, the range of entry points is slightly larger. As shown in Figure 30-B, the ball can sneak in close to the bottom of the half-cup you see from behind the ball, and it can sneak it near the very back, on the far side of the cup, as it comes down from above the hole. The range of possible entry points spans three-quarters of the cup.

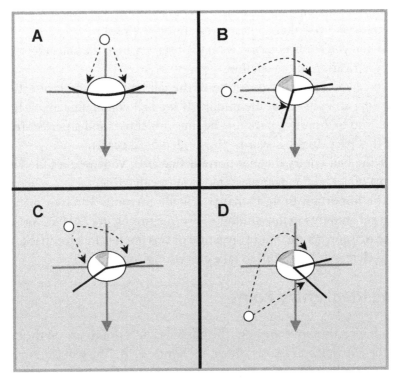

Figure 30: Ideal Entry Points

Halfway between them is the ideal entry point. If the entry point at the top of the cup is north, and the ball is coming from the west, in theory the ideal entry point is northwest. But since a ball on the high side has a better chance of dropping in than one on the low side, the point of maximum probability (no chance of lip-out, minimum effect of bumps) is actually higher than that, in the arc between north and northwest, the shaded area in the diagram. For a diagonal putt from above the hole, the range of entry points always includes the half of the cup you see, combined with the top half of the cup, as shown in Figure 30-C. However, as the ball's position moves from the cross line to above the hole on the fall line, the range of possible entry points reduces from three-quarters of the cup to half the cup, and the range of the ideal entry points gradually reduces from nearly a quarter of the cup to "true north", that is, the same as in Figure 30-A.

(This analysis assumes that there is some slope. If you're on a flat surface, there is no "top half". In that case, the range of entry points is the half of the cup you see, and the ideal entry point is in the middle of that range, directly on your sight line.)

For a diagonal putt from below the hole, as shown in Figure 30-D, the range of ideal entry points gets *larger* as you move from the cross line to the fall line, until you get to the 45-degree diagonal—because, for a short distance and medium slope, a power putt could ignore the slope entirely and enter the ball on the lower part of the half-cup you see. On the other hand, a putt with less pace can trickle in from around the back.

For those putts, the arc of ideal entry points, where the ball has the maximum chance of dropping in regardless of speed or terrain, extends from the theoretical halfway point (west-northwest) to just short of the fall line (north-northwest).

As the ball moves farther south, closer to the fall line, the range of entry points reduces rapidly to the half-cup you can see, because the ball can no longer get above the hole before it goes in. Similarly, the arc of ideal entry points reduces from a large slice of the pie to a small sliver.

No wonder a putt from below the hole is easier to make than one above it. For one thing, the back of the cup acts as a "backstop" that keeps the ball in the cup over a larger range of speeds. For another, the cup is effectively larger, because there is a wider range of entry points at which the ball drops into the hole.

Summary:
The Keys to Putting

This section summarizes what you have learned. And if you haven't already, it's worth spending some time at the practice green with a ball ramp, just to prove things to yourself. Because knowing them removes any mystery about what your putt did, and why.

Green-Reading Principles

- *Find the fall line.*

  - This is first and foremost. Where will water go when it runs towards the hole, and when it runs away?

- *Watch every putt.*

  - The last inch or two of travel tells you exactly where the fall line is, on that part of the green. (So balls that come to rest near the hole are ideal.)

  - The rate at which the ball slows down gives you a clue about green speed. If it comes to a stop quickly, the green is slow. If it stops very slowly, the green is fast.

Target-Selection Principles

- *Find your ideal target.*

  - The best place to do that is from slightly below the cross line.

  - For a given distance from the hole, the target is the same, regardless of what angle you're coming from.

  - After finding the fall line, moving to the cross line to pick your target (in addition to watching other putts) is the best way to detect an "optical illusion" hole.

  - When you find an optical illusion hole, you have to trust your read or find a way for your eyes to see the actual break.

- *Be a bit conservative.*

  - You don't want to "give away the hole". So if the putt doesn't break that much, prefer a target that is at the edge of the cup, or inside it, to maximize the chances that it will drop in even if your line or speed is a little off.

  - For a putt with more break, if you're slightly low but your speed is good, the next putt will be straight uphill or close to it—the easiest putt there is to make, even from several feet. So from any significant distance, if you're in the vicinity of the hole and below it, it's a good putt.

Speed Principles

- *Putts from below the hole are the easiest to make.*

  - You have a wider range of speeds and angles, and the back of the cup acts as a backstop.

  - *But*, for any breaking putt (or chip) to have a chance, the ball has to go above the hole at *some* point during its travels (hence the need to select a good target).

- *Power putt when you're below the hole, near the fall line, and not too far away.*

  ○ From up to around 3 feet away, you can take the break out of the equation, and make it a straight putt.

  ○ The slope will keep a miss from going too far, and the backstop at the back of the cup will work to keep a strong putt in the hole.

- *From any other location, and any greater distance, try to "die" the ball at the hole.*

  ○ That strategy gives you perfect feedback on your read and speed—from putt to putt, and from green to green.

  ○ Done well, your ball will tend to finish on the fall line below the hole, which is the easiest kind of putt there is to make.

Putt-Evaluation Principles

- *Feedback is essential.*

  ○ It is the only way you can improve.

  ○ But there are two dimensions to every putt—direction and velocity—and to get *useful* feedback, you need to know if the speed was off or the read and, in each case, by how much.

- *The sight line is always the READ line.*

  ○ For a continuous slope, the ball's distance directly above or below the sight line tells you *exactly* how far your read was off.

  ○ The distance above or below the sight line is the *exact distance* by which your read was off.

  ○ The target is constant for a given distance.

- *The cross line is the THRESHOLD for a makeable putt.*

  ○ To drop, the ball must reach or exceed the cross line, at some time in its travels. When the ball is already on the cross line, achieving that goal is trivial. But the closer the ball is to the fall line when you start, the more important that threshold becomes.

- *The fall line is always the SPEED line.*

  o If the ball finishes on the fall line, you had *perfect speed for the line you chose.* If your line was high, more force was needed to get the ball to the fall line than it would have taken to get it to the hole. If your line was low, less force was needed. In either case, the amount of force was perfect for that particular line.

  o The perpendicular distance to the fall line is the *exact distance* by which your speed was off for the line you chose. That feedback is about as much as you can get when your line is off, so file it away and move on.

  o Speed is the most important factor in putting, so the goal is to finish with the ball on the fall line, every time.

Reminder:

If you came here to preview the evaluation principles, be sure to return to The Science of Breaking Putts (page 74) after you finish, to understand *why* these principles work.

Self-Evaluation Principles

- *Close is good.*

  o Neither your speed nor your read has to be perfect. From any significant distance, coming within a few feet of the ideal target puts you within a few feet of the hole!

  o If you've been watching, you know exactly where the fall line is and exactly how fast the green is. So, for the second putt, *every 3-footer is makeable.*

- *You will learn, and you will improve.*

  o With sufficient repetition, you *will* master the putting game. You can't help it really. It's in your DNA. Your ancestors survived because they were good at that kind of thing. You're good at that kind of thing, too. Just give yourself a little time, and keep taking the feedback you need from every putt you see and every one you stroke. It will happen.

The Importance of Feedback (Once Again)

You now know how to get very precise feedback from every putt you make. From now on, you will know if you had the right read, and therefore chose the right line, *and* you will know if you had the right speed when you made the stroke.

Why is that feedback important? Well, as mentioned earlier, getting the right speed is the most critical factor in putting. The feedback you take from each putt tells you whether it was too slow or too fast for a particular hole—*regardless* of the line you chose. In other words, your line may have been way off, but you could *still* get accurate feedback on your speed—and that feedback is what allows you to gauge green speed. (As long as the greens are consistent, that is. Remember those professionals on that one unusual day!)

When you *know for certain* if your putt was slow or fast, and how fast or slow it was, you are in position to make adjustments. Similarly, knowing whether your choice of line was high or low—and *by exactly how much*—gives you the feedback you need to adjust your reads for those greens, on that day.

Maybe the green was fast, so the putt broke more than expected for the amount of slope you saw. Or maybe, you never really aimed high enough for the amount of slope that was there, even with average green speeds. Either way, the feedback you get on your choice of line tells you *what you need to know* to make better choices. With that feedback, you will find yourself dialing in good reads in no time. And that capability will pay dividends on every chip and every putt, throughout the round.

When you learn to derive that feedback, the first thing you'll notice is that your practice gets a lot better. I like to putt 3 balls at a time from any given position, using the first two to "dial in" the third. I recommend that approach.

As you get better at taking feedback, the first putt tells you what adjustments you need to make. The second putt tells you how well you made those adjustments. Perhaps the first sign of serious improvement is that you then frequently sink the third!

Over time, you'll find that the first ball is coming closer and closer—a sign that your reading skills have improved—and that the second ball is pretty well dialed in—a sign that your ability to adjust is in place—and that the third follows in the tracks of the second—a sign that your putting skills are repeatable.

As you notice yourself getting better on the practice green, you'll find that your putting improves on the course, as well. On the putting green, naturally, the feedback is *immediate*, and you play the *identical* putt with the second and third balls. But that sequence gives you just enough repetition to hone your green-reading and putt-feedback skills, along with your putting stroke.

During your round, you'll be deriving the same feedback to judge the pace of your putts and your initial read. Both of those factors are affected by green speed, so your feedback process is giving you a *feel* for the greens. Using that feel, you should begin to notice a dramatic difference in your results throughout the round. Even if you take the same *number* of putts, you should begin to notice that your initial putts are coming much closer, and that subsequent putts are much easier.

So go forth and putt! And may your 1-putts always outnumber your 3-putts!

**May your 1-putts always
outnumber your 3-putts!**

Part III

///

Green Reading

THIS SECTION TELLS YOU how to read a green with precision, so you can anticipate how the ball is going to move on different slopes.

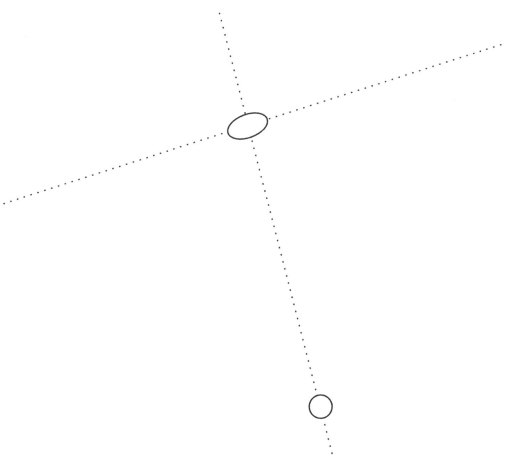

Reading
the Contours

Now that you know how to analyze a putt on a single slope, it's time to examine the kinds of greens you see in reality—contoured greens composed of multiple slopes and curves.

The good news is that principles of putt analysis remain the same on a putting surface composed of multiple slopes. Whether the line you chose was high or low, and whether your speed was fast or slow, can all be determined from the ball's finishing position. There is no difference at all when it comes to evaluating the *results* of your putt.

However, when the putting surface is made up of multiple curved slopes, picking the right *target* to aim at is more complex. While feedback on your speed is ultimately the most important, you also want to know how to chose the line.

This chapter shows how the ball's path is affected by curved slopes, and what happens as the ball moves from one slope to another. In general, we are concerned with the shape of the slope above the hole, and how that shape affects target selection. Learning how to read those contours will greatly improve your target selection process.

What follows is a way of naming or classifying the different kind of slopes and slope-combinations you're likely to encounter. This means when you come to a new green, you will have the ability to recognize its general type and have an idea how the ball will react.

A general framework of this kind will make it much easier for you to focus on a specific target to aim at. Doing this well is an art. As with any art, the more you practice, the more you learn. And the more you learn, the better you get.

Single-Slope Curves

Rarely will you find a slope that is perfectly consistent, unless you are dealing with a short putt. (That is one reason that short putts are easier.) If the slope isn't flat, it has to be one of two kinds shown in Figure 31:

- **Concave**
  A concave slope (think "cave" or "cavity") is flatter near the hole, and steeper away from it. With this kind of slope, a putt to a target farther away from the hole breaks significantly more than one closer in. The good news is that this arrangement gives you a wider range of targets that will work.

- **Convex**
  A convex surface (think "bubble", or maybe "vexing"!) is one that is steeper near the hole, and flatter away from it. On this kind of hole, a putt that is far away from the hole may not break very much at all, while one that is close may break far too much. Target selection has to be very precise on this kind of slope.

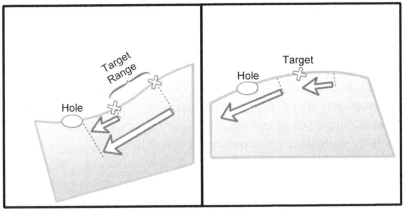

Concave Slope: Multiple Targets   Convex Slope: Single Target

Figure 31: Curved Slopes

These are the two types of curved individual slopes. In short, the concave ones are your friends. Convex slopes are less forgiving.

The remainder of this chapter deals with combinations of slopes, beginning with 2-slope combos, and then moving on to multiple-slope, "S-curve" combos.

2-Slope Combinations

When the ball encounters a different slope on its way to the hole, its path changes. Understanding exactly *how* it changes is the key to predicting the path it will take, so you can select an appropriate target.

The Uphill Wall

When a shallow slope meets a steeper slope (Figure 32), I call that a "wall". When a ball traveling across the green reaches the steeper slope, the ball runs on a flatter path. The gravity vector is stronger on the steep slope, so gravity pushes down on the ball with more force as it travels across the slope.

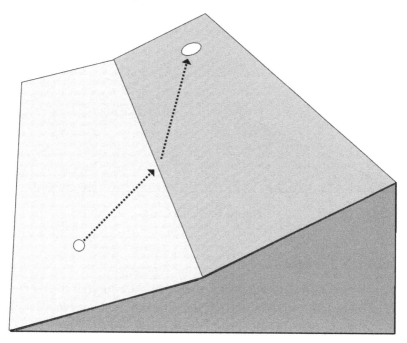

Figure 32: Uphill Wall

The Uphill Crest

This one tends to be surprising, until you get used to it. Here, the ball is running across a steeper slope, until it reaches the crest, where the slope becomes shallower (Figure 33).

Because the gravity vector is weaker on the shallow slope, the ball runs on a *higher* line when it reaches the shallower slope. In effect, the ball appears to break "uphill" when it reaches the crest of the hill.

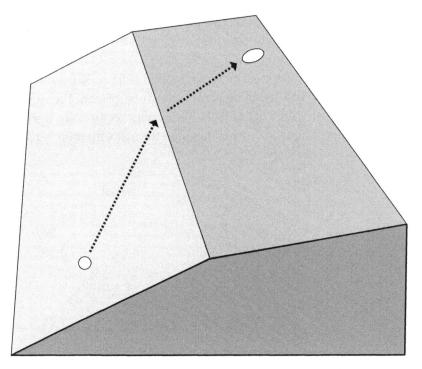

Figure 33: Uphill Crest

The Uphill Ridge

The ball goes uphill until it gets to the ridge. After that, it runs downhill. As it reaches the top of the ridge, the path changes to a higher line, as when reaching the crest of any steep slope. However, there are two alternatives after that. If the ball has the perfect speed to just barely reach the top of the ridge, it runs straight downhill from there. If it has slightly more speed, it carries on past the top a little way, curving more and more and more until eventually (if the slope is steep enough), it runs straight downhill (see the two alternate paths in Figure 34).

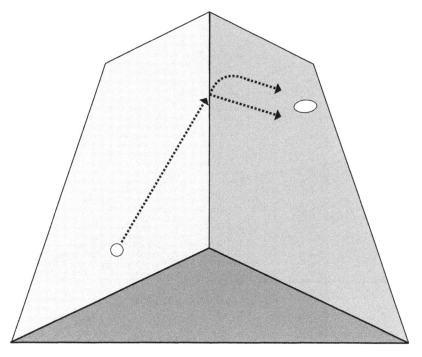

Figure 34: Uphill Ridge

The Downhill Shelf

This situation occurs a lot on multi-tier greens. You're on a fairly level surface that is going slightly downhill towards a lower tier, but at the edge of the "shelf" you're on, there is a steep drop-off down to the next tier (Figure 35).

As the ball travels across the divide, it takes a sharp turn when it reaches the edge and plunges downhill. The direction the ball takes depends on its speed when it reaches the edge (assuming it's going fast enough to get there). If it is going very fast, the ball simply travels at an increased angle—so if it was going 45 degrees away from you when it reached the edge, it may be going at a 60-degree angle down the hill.

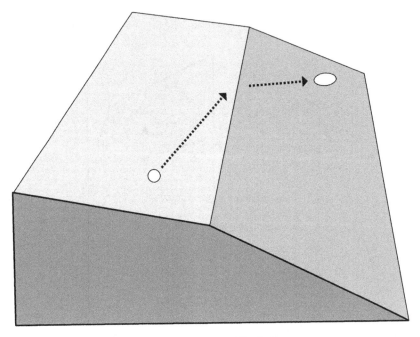

Figure 35: Downhill Shelf

There are two ways to play this kind of hole. If the hill is steep enough that a ball placed at the edge will roll down and reach the cup, imagine a "virtual cup" at the point directly above the hole. Putt the ball to exactly that spot. When the ball reaches that spot it should have just enough momentum to carry it over the edge. Then gravity will do the rest of the work and take the ball to the hole. (Tiger Woods did that once on the 17th "island" green at the TPC Sawgrass course, holing a miraculous long-distance putt from very far away.)

The alternative is to play the putt with more speed, which means it will have a shallow arc as it goes to the edge, and a steeper arc after it goes over. Taking these two arcs into account, play the ball to a target on the fall line above the hole but below the edge of the shelf.

Either way, speed control needs to be precise to make this kind of putt, or even to leave the ball anywhere near the hole. That is what makes a putt from a shelf so tricky.

The Downhill Ramp

This one is like the off-ramp from a freeway (Figure 36). From a steep slope where the ball is moving rapidly downhill, the ball encounters a shallower slope where it gradually slows. Because there is less gravity pushing the ball downhill, the ball runs on a flatter line when it reaches the shallower slope.

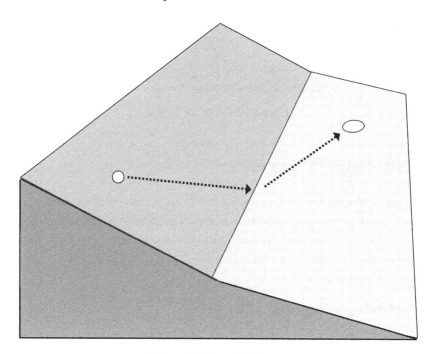

Figure 36: Downhill Ramp

The Downhill Valley

Here, a downhill slope meets an uphill slope (Figure 37). As it gets to the bottom of the valley, the ball initially runs on a flatter line. After that, gravity is stronger, pushing the ball down towards the bottom of the slope.

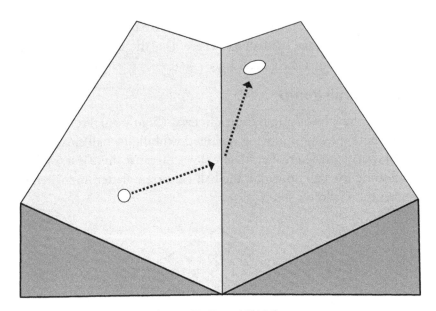

Figure 37: Downhill Valley

Multi-Slope "S-Curves"

As you will know if you've encountered one, a multi-slope green is an even tougher prospect than two slopes. The double break makes the ball curve first in one direction, and then in the opposite direction. On roads, such double bends are known as *S-curves*. They are tricky but not impossible.

The Valley S-Curve

This kind of double-breaking curve is the easiest to see. Figure 38 shows a slope coming in from the left at the start of the putt, joining one that comes in from the right later on, at a different angle.

It's fairly easy to see the ball banking off the slope on the left, running up the slope on the right, and then banking off that one as it travels on down to the hole.

The faster the putt, the farther down the initial slope the ball will travel before it gets to the second slope. From there, the ball's remaining momentum will carry it onward. The trick is to identify the "crux"—the point at which the ball will cross over from one slope to another, with just enough momentum to reach the hole.

Once you've identified the crux, you treat it like the hole, and choose a target that will get the ball to *that point*. The difference is that instead of dying the ball at that point, you want the ball to reach it with sufficient momentum to carry on down the hill to the hole.

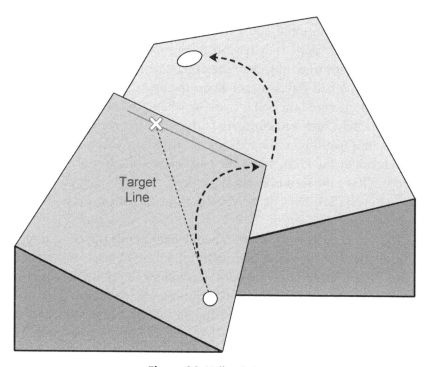

Figure 38: Valley S-Curve

As with every other breaking putt, speed is critical. The good news is that a ball traveling too fast tends to run farther up the second slope, which slows it down. So these putts tend to have enough leeway to make you look like a genius!

(I had one such putt on the 17th hole at Del Monte, in Monterey, CA. I saw the ball coming off of one slope, rolling on to another, and then coming off that. I then putted the ball perfectly down the S-curve, rolling it in from 30 feet. Made my day!)

You'll find that your ability to visualize a "serpentine" break improves as you improve your ability to see the break on any single slope.

The Hilltop S-Curve

You've already seen the kind of curve that occurs when you putt over a ridge. It's the opposite of a valley, and I called it an uphill ridge (Figure 34), but we could also call it a "hilltop curve". It becomes an S-curve because the putt changes direction near the top of the ridge where the slope is flatter (breaking "uphill") and then changes direction again when it gets to the other side of the ridge. Here the direction the ball travels depends on the angle of the slope at that point and the speed the ball is carrying when it gets there.

Fortunately, such situations are fairly rare. They're also difficult to depict in a two-dimensional diagram! Just know that you'll see the first break at the crest, when the ball reaches the top of the ridge, and you'll see the second break at the shelf, when the ball reaches the downhill on the other side. So you'll picture the path as a crest-break, followed by a shelf-break.

The flatter the hill, the more time the ball spends traveling across the shelf at the top, on a path determined by its pace and by the point where it crested. That path determines the point at which it reaches the edge of the shelf. At that point, its path is determined mostly by the way the slope is facing on that part of the hill, and at a pace that is determined mostly by the speed of the green and the degree of slope.

Visualizing the multiple breaks and curving paths is, naturally, quite a difficult task. If the far slope is steep enough, the best way to proceed is to pick the spot on the far side of the hill where a ball will roll to the hole, and aim for the ball to "die" at that spot.

That is another advantage of the "die at the hole" putting technique. The better you are at getting the ball to travel a precise distance, the better chance you have of making this shot.

Of course, you'll want to carry just a *tiny* bit of extra speed in this case, to be sure the ball topples over the far side of the ridge. But that is the easiest way to make the shot.

Even when you see the shot, though, your pace needs to be precise for the ball to follow the predicted path. Your goal, in a situation of this kind, is just to get the ball somewhere near the hole!

The Roller Coaster S-Curve

When you putt through a valley and then over a ridge, or vice-versa, I call that a "roller coaster" S-curve. Again, this kind of situation doesn't come up too often—which is great news, because the ball's path is once again difficult to visualize. When it does come up, it helps to know what the individual breaks will do—but to take advantage of that information, as with most of the slope situations discussed in this chapter, speed control needs to be precise.

Getting a Break

You know how to read a green, find your target, and get the right feedback from each putt you make. You're on your way to mastering the putting game. This chapter gives you additional information to help you hone your green-reading skills, identify which way the ball is going to break, and by how much.

One Target to Rule Them All

In this section, we discover why, whatever it looks like to the eye, the ideal target is always the same, no matter what angle you are putting from. The target depends on the speed of the green, the degree of slope, and your distance from the hole—but it does *not* depend on the angle you're coming from.

When we talked about downhill sliders in "Vertical and Diagonal Putts", we noted that they appear to break more than any other putt, because the ball starts moving downhill so quickly. However, that effect is only an illusion.

While the ball is moving, the effect of surface friction is minimal. With friction minimized, gravity acts on the ball. The force that initially breaks the surface friction is your putt. The friction is still there, though. Eventually, it slows the ball down and brings it to rest. At that point, gravity stops acting on it. As long as the ball is moving, there are two forces at work: gravity and the force of your putt. At the beginning, your putt is the strongest force. At the end, as the ball is slowing, gravity is the strongest force.

When you putt uphill, your putting force is necessarily stronger. It dominates the equation. When you putt downhill, you putt with less force. That brings gravity into the equation more quickly. When the downhill slope is steep and the green is fast, you need to putt with *very* little force. In that situation, the ball begins to break the moment it leaves the putter head—which gives the impression that it is "sliding" downhill.

The reality is that the amount of break does *not* change just because of the angle the ball is coming from. The ball *appears* to be breaking more, because you have to putt more slowly, so gravity takes effect that much sooner.

In fact, on a green that is steep enough and fast enough, the ball can be seen to break the moment it leaves the putter. A sure sign that the green has a *lot* of break in it. (In most cases, that is also a sure sign that you needed to putt on a *much* higher line, to compensate for the speed of the green and the slope.)

We have already noted that you putt with more force going uphill, and with less force downhill, which changes the rate at which gravity takes effect. Because of the difference in ball speeds, the uphill putt goes relatively straight for much of its length, and hooks towards the hole at the end, without ever coming near the ideal target.

The downhill putt, on the other hand, has a much flatter trajectory that takes it closer to the ideal target on its way to the hole. This creates the illusion that the downhill putt breaks more than the uphill putt.

That effect is only illusion.

Optical illusions can be pretty darn persistent, though. And this particular illusion has caused at least one noted analyst to conclude that you need to allow more break for an uphill putt, and less for a downhill putt. But the fact of the matter is that the ideal target from a given distance does not change just because of the angle the putt is coming from.

The location of the ideal target *does* depend on distance, because gravity is acting on the ball for a longer period of time for a longer putt. But the location does *not* depend on the *angle* of the putt.

From the same distance, the ideal target remains the same for an uphill, downhill, or sidehill putt—something you can prove for yourself with a simple experiment.

To do the experiment, find a hole that is sitting on a consistent slope and find the fall line. Find a spot on the cross line from which you can roll a breaking ball into the hole. Then mark your point of aim on the fall line.

Next, move below the cross line, aim at the same target, and incrementally increase your speed. If you start with the same speed you used from the cross line, the first thing you'll notice is that the ball always stops on your sight line to the hole. As you increase speed by starting with the ball farther up the ramp, the ball will get closer and closer to the hole, always stopping on your sight line to the hole, until eventually it drops into the hole.

Finally, move up the slope and reduce velocity as you aim at the target. Again, you'll notice that the ball always stops on the sight line to the hole and, with the right velocity, lands in the hole.

Once you figure out how much the putt is going to break for a given distance from the hole, the target remains the same—no matter what angle you're looking at it from. Knowing that, you can pick your target from the angle that is easiest for you to see, and then use that target from wherever you are putting from.

I like to stand below the hole to find the fall line. But I think it is easiest to see the amount of break from just below the cross line. And double-checking your read in that manner has the advantage that if the hole has a different break than you thought it did (an "optical illusion" hole, discussed later), you're more likely to spot it.

When to Choose a Faster Line

As explained in the section, Uphill Putts Are Easiest, the back of the cup acts as a backstop when you are below the hole. And the steeper the slope, the more effective that backstop is. You can take a straighter, faster line to the hole, because a putt that is too fast can still work, thanks to the backstop. (The die-at-the-hole target is the same, but the speed needs to be more precise.)

Distance and Gravity

As we have seen in this section, gravity is constant for a given distance from the hole. But friction holds the ball in place on the green. When the ball isn't moving, the size of the gravity vector is a big fat zero. It is only when the force of the putt overcomes friction that gravity takes effect.

A longer putt takes more force, so friction is overcome for a longer period of time. The farther you are from the hole, the longer gravity plays a role. In essence, then, the gravity vector is slightly stronger when you are farther from the hole—and the faster the green, the stronger it is.

Still, from the standpoint of reading your putt (the main point of this book), the difference is too subtle to matter. It only matters if you're a physics nerd, and you're making precise measurements!

In addition, taking advantage of the backstop and putting with more force reduces the chances of coming up short.

From below the hole then, there are multiple combinations of targets and speeds that work just fine. That is one reason that putts from below the hole are so much easier than putts from above it.

But while you can afford a missed putt that is a little fast going uphill, you can't afford that kind of miss going downhill. So, for a downhill putt, you want to be conservative. Aim for the ideal target—the one farthest from the hole—and plan to die the ball at the hole. Because then, if your line is a little off, you still have a short tap-in to finish the hole.

Finally, putting to the ideal target gives you precise feedback on your read and speed. If you intentionally choose a flatter, faster line, and you miss, you not only race by the hole farther than you otherwise would have, but there is little you can learn from the putt.

In summary:

1. The power-putt philosophy makes sense when you can eliminate the break and make it a straight putt (that is, when you are below the hole, near the fall line, and not too far away).

2. From above the hole, to the side of it, or from far away, you must play for the ideal target and get the speed right.

3. If there is *any doubt at all* about your ability to hole out the putt, you should choose the ideal target and aim to die the ball at the hole. That choice gives the best possible second putt, and gives you the most accurate feedback.

4. If you are *confident* in your ability to make the putt (you are not too far away), and *a miss won't hurt you much* (you're going uphill, and you're near the fall line), you can choose a flatter line to straighten out the putt.

When Break Doesn't Matter

In the tips section of The Putting Zone, Geoff Magnum makes an interesting point about putts that are near the hole and below the cross line, between 8:00 and 4:00:

> Putts from that angle that are 'within the leather' (between the bottom of the grip and the bottom of the club, or within 2 feet of the hole) almost never have enough break to cause the golfer much concern about the pace or line of the putt. Just knock it in, perhaps favoring the high side of the inside of the cup. Don't worry about babying it or ramming it home, just make a nice firm roll into the cup.

Note that you're not trying to power-putt those shots, in an effort to "take the break out." It's just that you don't have to concern yourself much with the break. You can usually just aim "high and inside", and putt to that target.

He goes on to say that you really don't want to be thinking about "taking the break out", because on any longer putt, or from any higher than 8:00 to 4:00, that approach is a recipe for disaster.

Optical Illusions: Putts that Break Uphill

Don't you just hate it when you *know* a putt will break one way, and it breaks in the opposite direction entirely? I know I do. I've seen it happen a few times, and it drives me nuts. I'm standing there and I can see the break, clear as day. Then I make my putt (or, if I'm lucky, someone else putts first) and I see the ball break opposite to the way I expected.

The third hole at Pebble Beach is like that. Standing on the green with the ocean to your left, you can very clearly see the slope running downhill to your right, towards the fairway. Then you putt the ball and watch it break 180 degrees opposite to that, towards the ocean! And no matter how long you stare at it, *knowing* which way it will break, all you *see* is the break going the other way.

I was fortunate to find an example of that illusion on a practice green near my home, where I could take my time and examine it closely. From the far end of the green, facing the pro shop, the major slope of the green is to the left. But from that position, you can also see a ridge running at a diagonal through the green, with a minor slope to the right.

The hole location was just to the right of that ridge.

Standing at the top of the green, facing the pro shop, the edge of the green on the right is *clearly* lower than the hole. The hole is tilted slightly in that direction, as well, and a marker placed a foot or so to the right of the hole can be seen to be slightly below the level of the hole. Clearly, the putt breaks to the right.

So I pick a target 6 inches to the left of the hole, putt, and watch the ball break even further left! Educated, I putt to the right of the hole, and watch it break left, straight "uphill" towards the hole!

Weird. I go over to the left side of the hole. I find that I am now standing well below the hole, with a steeply sloping green, coming my way. Okay, mystery solved. That is the real fall line.

I go back to my original location, now knowing for sure that the green slopes to the left. But when I get there, and look at the putt, I still *see* it breaking to the right!

I spent 10 minutes on that hole, walking back and forth. Standing to the left of the hole, I could see a steep slope coming my way. Standing behind my ball, I could see a slope going *right*. It was a shallower slope, to be sure. But it was unmistakable. I could see the slope going left *behind* the hole, but *at* the hole all I could see was the slope going right. I'd try a few putts, watch them break left, then look at the hole. I *still* saw the slope going right. I saw the hole tilted to the right, and I saw my marker slightly below the hole on the right. I knew in my head that it went left. I saw balls *going* left. But looking at it, I could only see it sloping to the right.

Clearly, the effect was an optical illusion. But it was a good one! No amount of *telling* myself that the ball goes left could make me *imagine* the ball going that way. Even after watching balls break to the left—several times!—I still *saw* the green breaking to the right.

This same illusion is responsible for several "mystery house" venues around the country. They build a house on the side of a hill, sloping so steeply that you need a handrail to hold onto as you move around. They'll put a table in that house that is clearly angled away from the wall, down towards the floor. Then you'll watch, mystified, as a can of soda rolls up the table and out the window! In your head, you know you are leaning towards the window, but what you *see* is the table sloping away from it. Intellectually, you know that the slope of the table isn't as severe as the slope of the floor. But that information is in your head, and it just isn't making it to your eyes.

That kind of illusion can make it difficult to read a green. In the remaining sections of this chapter, we'll discuss ways to offset that effect.

Walk Around the Hole—*Sometimes*

One way to counteract the optical illusion effect is to walk all the way around the hole, to make *sure* you know which way the putt will break.

If you do see a big break in one direction, and a smaller break in a different direction, you can figure out which one predominates. Then (this is the hard part) get behind your ball, *ignore* what you see when you look at the putt, and place your bet on the putt moving in the predicted direction. (If *everywhere* you stand seems to be downhill from the hole, it's really tough. The best thing you can do at that point is find the edge of the green that is lowest, and expect the ball to break in that direction.)

Walking all the way around the hole is one way to find the actual break. You see the pros doing that all the time. And with the money they have on the line, it makes sense. But dang it all, we weekend golfers just cannot afford the time it takes for four golfers to walk all the way around every hole, laboriously lining up every putt, when the fact of the matter is that it just doesn't make that much difference. The pros generally play in *pairs*, too, not foursomes—so they have time we don't have.

That's why, earlier, I suggested the idea of standing below the hole to establish the fall line. The longer you can stand there as others putt, the more accurate your read will be. If you then see the ball break uphill, you know that you chose the wrong fall line! At that point, you should move around to find the real fall line, mentally recalibrate to pick a target, and ignore what your eyes are telling you when you step up to the putt.

When it really matters—putting for a rare birdie, or when you actually have a chance to win the dadgum tournament—walk around the hole to be sure you know which way the putt is going to break. But that should be the exception, rather than the rule.

Speed Saves

If you are the first to putt, you're the guinea pig. Your playing partners give you information with *their* putts. It's only right that you return the favor. So pick a spot above the hole on what you think is the fall line, make your best putt, and learn from the result.

Remember: Putting with the right *speed* is way more important than putting on the right line. With good speed, you end up directly below the hole, every time. And a ball directly below the hole is (as we've said a few times) the easiest putt there is—it's simple to line up, and there is a wide range of speeds at which the ball drops. Your work on speed control will therefore pay off in highly makeable second putts, even when your initial read is off.

Therefore, it is important to work on *speed* with every putt you make—and by "work on speed," I mean take the right feedback from each putt, so you know exactly how far the ball went past the hole, or how far short of the hole you left it. Assuming the greens are consistent, that information will turn you into a 2-putt wizard, who invariably makes the "come-backer".

Share Knowledge

Another thing we can do, as weekend golfers, is to share local knowledge. When there is an optical illusion hole, tell the people you're playing with. Yeah, if you are playing with others, your chances of winning are reduced by an infinitesimal amount. But if you keep people from agonizing over every putt, you have a 100% chance of making the round go faster, which makes the round more fun for everyone—including the people behind you.

Bob for Breaks?

I can't say that plumb-bobbing is my absolute favorite technique in the world, but when your head is telling you one thing, and your eyes are telling you another, it was worth investigating, as a way of convincing your eyes to believe your head.

The idea behind the technique is that if you hold the grip of the club lightly between two fingers, the shaft will hang down vertically, like a weight on the end of a string (a plumb-bob).

The point of the technique is to help you read the break in the green. But how does it work exactly? It's true the center of the shaft will be vertical, but the shaft itself is tapered, so it doesn't give you a "true vertical" to compare things with—unless you angle it just right.

One helpful article I found on the web points out that if you angle the putter head just right, the edge of the shaft will be vertical—something you can check by holding the putter next to a door frame, for example. With my putter, I found that with the edge of the putter head running towards the door, the shaft is angled well to the right. With the putter head facing me, the shaft angles well to the left. Midway between those two positions, with the putter head at a 45-degree angle, the shaft is pretty close to vertical. Practicing beforehand can, then, help you consistently reproduce the angle.

The author of that article says that (in theory) if you stand behind the ball on the sight line, and hold the putter so it lines up with the ball, the hole will be on the left if the green breaks that way, and it will be on the right if the green breaks to the right.

However, he also says that it is quite possible to go wrong with this technique and, in the end, he concludes that, "while one might have some fun experimenting with this technique in playing by oneself or in practice on the putting green, that time expended far outweighs any benefits gained". After experimenting myself, I am forced to agree with that assessment.

Another idea I have experimented with takes advantage of the fact that when the putter is vertical, the bottom of the grip is perfectly horizontal. To use that information, you need to hold the putter by the grip, rather than holding the shaft at the bottom of the grip, as when plumb-bobbing normally. Then raise your arm so the bottom edge of the grip is at eye level. Voila! You now have a (very small) horizontal surface to compare the hole with. If the hole slopes left in comparison with that line, that's the way the green breaks.

The goal is to offset the effect of the optical illusion that tells us the green breaks to the right, when it actually breaks left. We can't *see* that break, because we are effectively inside the mystery house. We may be aware that the entire house (the green) is tilted in one direction, but all our eyes see is the table (the area around the green) tilted in the other.

Having a perfectly vertical and perfectly horizontal surface to compare with gives you a chance to see what your brain is telling you, which can help you trust that information. It is really darn hard to trust the green is breaking one way, when your eyes are telling you something totally different, and even your feet may also be giving you false signals. The plumb-bob technique might help—except when it doesn't. More about that next.

Trust Your Read (not your "bob")

Once you've found the target for the putt (ideally from a position at right angles to the fall line), it is important to *trust* your read when you get behind the ball. Because things can look a lot different from that perspective.

When you're behind the ball, lots of optical-illusion factors can come into play. And when they do, trusting your eyes can create problems. So it's important to trust the read you made when you were in the best possible position to make it.

**Trust your read—
but NOT from behind the ball.**

Plumb-bobbing is intended as way to overcome the optical illusions, but as the story in the sidebar makes clear, I found it to be no help at all for that purpose.

Plumb-bobbing an Optical Illusion

I'd had some limited success with plumb-bobbing when I first started experimenting with it, but a few weeks later I saw its limitations. I was playing in a pro-am hosted by the NCGA at the Jack Nicklaus signature course Coyote Creek, south of San Jose. And there I found a true optical illusion hole.

(continued on next page)

• • •

Coming up to the hole, Bill Troyanoski (my pro) pointed out the general slope of the terrain was to the left. (We were in a valley, with the highway uphill, to the right, and the creek far away in the middle of the valley, to the left.) At the same time, I could see that the green had a severe slope going to the right. I was thinking the green was on the side of a hill, at that point, and in fact there was a ridge running through the green.

As with most of the optical illusion holes I've encountered, the hole was near the top of that ridge. Maybe it's the lack of a visible slope behind the hole that throws off the eye. Anyway, I found the fall line while watching the others putt, and it was definitely to the left (from where my ball was) down towards the creek.

Then I got behind my ball. The break looked as if it was *definitely* going to the right. The slope was going right, and when I tried the plumb-bobbing technique, *the hole was angled to the right*, as well.

I double checked. I went back to the fall line. Standing to the left of the hole, down the fall line, I was significantly lower than when I was standing behind the ball. From behind the ball, my feet were almost level with the hole, with only a mild uphill to get there.

I decided to ignore my eyes, trust my read, and play for the ball to break left. It did, and I made the putt. So much for plumb-bobbing. I wish I could tell you why it didn't work. I honestly don't know. All I know for sure is that the plumb-bob technique conformed to the optical illusion, rather than the reality.

Besides the limitations of plumb-bobbing, that experience taught me that you need to pick a target from the cross line, and to keep that target in mind as you move to the ball. Then putt to that target—*regardless* of what your eyes are telling you from behind the ball.

For me, that seems to be the only reliable way to triumph over an optical illusion.

On the other hand, my pro partner had no trouble seeing the slope to the left in the larger terrain. He observed it as we were riding up the green, and knew it was there all along. But I couldn't see what he saw. All I could see was the slope to the right in the micro-terrain—and that's what I saw as we were approaching the hole, as well.

Perhaps there is a way to acquire his ability. Or perhaps there is an intrinsic difference between "big picture" people (he would be one), and those of us who tend to focus on details. I am in the latter camp. Each has its strengths, but a detail-oriented focus is certainly no help when attempting to combat an optical illusion!

So, at the moment, the best weapon in my personal arsenal is the ability to trust my read. But I'd sure love to find a way to *see* the break, instead of having to *believe* the break, despite the evidence of my eyes!

Part IV

//

Going Deeper

THIS SECTION COVERS special situations, the "yips", and the mental game. Special situations include:

- What to do when you can't find the break
- How to proceed when you've missed by a mile
- Reading chips
- The effect of grain
- "False greens" where a ball won't stay at rest

Special Situations

This chapter gives you some additional tools for when you find yourself in the "special situations" that are endemic to golf: finding the break on a multi-slope green; what to do when you miss by a mile; a few words on how to read your chips; how to read and putt on different grains; the hazards of false greens; and the yips and how to cure them. (So, yes, they're more like "standard situations", but the chapter title needed more zip!)

Can't Find the Break

Sometimes, you look at the hole from one angle, and you swear it breaks one way. But when you look at it from a somewhat different angle, you'll swear it breaks a different way. Why? Because the green has a *combination* of slopes. How then do you get a reliable read?

One solution is to walk in an arc between those two angles, always keeping the same distance from the hole. As you walk, be very aware of your feet and their relation to the hole. You should feel yourself moving down in one direction, up in the other. With luck, you'll notice that your feet are somewhat lower in one location, relative to the hole. If so, that is the location of the actual fall line.

**If there are multiple low points,
walk an arc between them to find the lowest.**

If you still can't decide which point is lower, get down closer to the ground. One of the things that can throw us off is that when standing, our eyes are always well above the hole. When locations are at nearly the same level, a subtle difference can be difficult to detect when your eyes are so far above the hole.

If you're somewhere near 6 feet tall, and you're 6 to 10 feet away, it can be difficult to discern a difference of a few inches. Getting your eyes down closer to your feet can make such differences easier to see.

**To get a clearer picture of the real slope,
get your eyes closer to your feet.**

You'll see pros getting down behind their ball all the time. It helps them see the way the slope is actually running. Once they do that, they're better able to pick a target to aim at.

Squatting down behind your ball isn't necessary if other putts have already given you the read. But if you're putting first, or others have putted out without giving you a read, it's a good tool to have in your bag.

Missed by a Mile

Every once in a while, a putt will surprise you. You're standing there, thinking the ball will break one way, and it goes somewhere else entirely. The problem is simple: you *thought* you saw the fall line, but you were wrong. The slope was undoubtedly there, but it was another slope that was "dominating the equation", so to speak. And that slope was the *actual* fall line.

The last inch of travel always shows you the actual fall line. If you're watching someone else's putt, the first thing you want to do is to move over to that line, to see the hole from that angle.

But anytime you miss by a lot, it's a good time to walk around the hole.

After a bad miss, walk around the hole.

When you miss by a wide margin, it is usually the case that one of two things happened:

1. You were thinking of something else as you made the putt. Instead of holding a mental picture of your *target*, your mind was elsewhere. Lacking intent, the putt happened almost at random.

2. You didn't have the right fall line. Your putt may have been just right for the line you saw, but it was definitely wrong for the putt you were making.

In either case, walking around the hole gives you a chance to reset your internal systems. If your concentration slipped, it gives you a chance to gather yourself. If your read was off, it gives you a chance to identify the true fall line. And in addition to giving you information you need for the *next* putt, it gives you the all-important feedback you need for the *previous* one.

If you're just beginning to play the game, big misses will happen a lot. Don't worry about it.

But if you've been playing for a while, and have developed the habit of sizing up each putt with an evaluation like, "too fast" or "too low", your first reaction will probably be to blame yourself, saying something like "bad read *and* bad speed". Don't do that. Instead, realize that you were most likely fooled by what you *thought* you saw, and that you didn't find the actual fall line. Everything starts with knowing where the fall line is. If you get that wrong, nothing else works.

Finding the actual fall line in that situation tells you that your initial read of the green was wrong, and *that* is the skill that needs to improve. Without that knowledge, you could wind up making the wrong adjustment on future putts—especially with respect to speed.

If you have thousands of dollars riding on each putt, like the pros, by all means walk around the hole on every putt, to be sure you found the actual fall line. You might want to do that if you have a par or birdie in sight, as well.

But if there isn't a whole lot at stake, please don't hold up the game by walking around the hole on every single putt! Instead, make the best read you can, as efficiently as you can.

Most of the time, your read won't be far off, and the ball will end up reasonably close to where you're aiming, ready for the finishing putt. But on those rare occasions when a putt takes you completely by surprise, it's time to walk around to the line the putt showed you, to get a second opinion.

Reading Your Chips

I'll have a lot more to say about chipping and pitching in the next book in this series. The important point to make here is that to pick a *target* for your chip, you apply the same green-reading skills you use for putting. Even more importantly, you use the same *analysis* skills to evaluate the results of your chip—not only to improve your chipping and green-reading skills, but to get the information you need for your next putt.

To do that, you'll finish the chip the same way you finish a putt. You'll tilt your head as the ball leaves your field of vision, hold your body position until the ball comes to rest, and *evaluate the result*. Then you'll take feedback from that stroke to find out exactly where the fall line is, and to get a read on the amount of break to expect (a combination of green speed and slope). You will observe whether there was more or less break than you expected, and whether the ball landed above the hole or below it.

After you make that read, you are going to say to yourself something like "too low (or high) and too slow (or fast)", and let the information be processed by your mind-body computer for your next shot—hopefully, sinking the putt for an actual up and down. But at the very least, making a 2-putt for what is generally a good result for us—an amateur up and down.

The Effect of Grain

Some grasses like Bermuda have a grain, which is the direction in which the grass grows. I don't play on those grasses, so I'm not used to looking for the differences that tell you which way the grain is going. However, I can offer some quick advice on how to pick up the grain and, more importantly, how to use that information to help your putting.

When the grass is growing towards you, you're looking into the grain. You see the ends of the grasses, so the color is flat and dark—like you're looking into a brush. When you're looking down grain, you see the shafts of the grass, and the color is light and shiny—like looking at long, straight hair.

In Getting Up and Down, greens-master Tom Watson recommends looking at the edges of the hole to see which way the grain is growing—there will be a slight overlap on one side, but not the other. That's great advice. In addition to its use when putting, you can use it just to see if the greens have any grain in the first place. (If the grass is growing evenly around the edges of the hole, you don't need to concern yourself. If it is over the lip on one side but not on the other, you do!)

For another illustration, check out the YouTube video Reading Grain On Bermuda Greens, which shows you some sample holes, and identifies the grain.

Okay, so you've worked out which way the grain is going, but what you really need to know is what effect it will have on your putts.

For starters, there are a few principles that are worth knowing, captured nicely in the online slideshow, Golf tips: The easy guide to reading the grain of a green:

1. A putt going *with* the grain moves 25% faster.

2. A putt *against* the grain moves 25% slower.

3. A putt *across* the grain curves in the direction of the grain.

4. As with slope, grain has the most effect at the end of the putt, when the ball is moving slowest.

But when you begin to work out the rules for taking feedback from a sidehill, cross-grain putt, things get complicated.

Let's start with a putt that is straight uphill or downhill. If the grain is going into you, the putt will be slower, as each blade of grass works to slow it down. Conversely, if the grain is going away from you, the putt will be faster. The green will be "slick" as the ball skids along the surface. In summary: Grain into you = slower, grain away from you = faster.

Grain into you = slower, grain away from you = faster.

Our very first conclusion is that grain causes a straight uphill or downhill putt to be faster or slower than another, depending on whether you are putting into it, or along it. And it will also make a difference if the grain is going at an angle. And if the grain is at right-angles to your putt, meanwhile, it shouldn't affect speed, but it will cause the ball to break!

Whew. And that's just straight putts. No wonder putting on a grained green is such an art.

Now let's take a look at a sidehill putt. If you are directly perpendicular to the fall line, and the grain is going uphill, there will be much less break. The ends of the "brush" work against gravity, increasing friction and preventing the ball from breaking.

If the grain is going downhill, the opposite is true. The ball will break more, because the slick surface gives less resistance to gravity.

To complicate matters, the grain generally won't be growing straight up or down relative to the fall line. It will likely be going at an angle, to produce a stronger or weaker effect. But at least that variation will be consistent. The bigger problem is that if you are not directly above, below, or across from the hole, there are opposite influences to account for.

For example, if the grain is going down the fall line and you're below the hole to the side, the grain going downward means the ball will break more, because there is less resistance to gravity. Meanwhile, to the degree you're putting into the grain, you'll need more speed. If you imagine the ball is 45 degrees below the hole, you'll need more break and more speed than you would on a grass that has no grain.

If the grain is going up the fall line, on the other hand, the ball will break less. So, from the same 45-degree position, you'll need less break and less speed than on grass with no grain.

On grass with no grain, there is only one rule:

- For a faster green, allow *more* break, and putt with *less* speed.

But for a green with grain, given what we now know, there are two *opposite* effects to consider, and therefore two rules:

- If the ball travels across an *uphill* grain, allow *less* break and putt with *less* speed.

- If the ball travels across a *downhill* grain, allow *more* break, and putt with *more* speed.

Figuring out the exact combination of factors in those circumstances is indeed a fine art. For any given putt, you have to decide if the slope or the grain will have the larger effect, and choose your target accordingly.

But the important thing is that you have to take the grain into account when you derive feedback from your putts. You'll get the same information as before: The putt was too fast or too slow; you allowed too much or too little break. But now, you have to *qualify* those observations, taking the grain into account.

For example:

- The putt was too fast, going down grain.

- The putt was too fast (or slow), going up grain.

- I allowed for too much (or little) break going with the grain.

- I allowed for too much (or little) break going against the grain.

It's going to take more putts to get a good feel for how things work in those circumstances. The take-away? Practice! It's a good idea to spend more time on the putting green before a round, working with different combinations of grain and slope until the mind-body computer has taken the conditions on board.

False Greens

There are some surfaces that are steep enough, with a low enough coefficient of friction, that a ball placed on the surface begins to move immediately and will not come to rest. That kind of surface is not really a "green". It's not a place that any ball can ever call home.

For example, some greens have what is called a "false front"—it looks like a green, but no ball ever comes to rest there. Of course, a wedge shot might roll back off a normal green because of backspin, but we're talking about something like the notorious 14th green at Augusta where, when you're watching the Masters on TV, you'll see *putts* that don't go far enough and then roll back off the green.

Areas of that kind *look* like they are part of the green. But they aren't. They are another hazard, really. You have to avoid that area to have any kind of chance on the hole. Depending on where they are, those areas could be called a false front, false back, or false side.

> **Note:**
>
> To my mind, such areas are manifestly unfair. If it *looks* like a green, it should *act* like a green! (I feel the same way about hidden hazards.)

One hole that is infamous for being almost totally unplayable in that regard is the 14th hole at Pebble Beach. It has a false front *and* a false back. Those areas are so large that the amount of green surface that is actually playable is about the size of a large pool table.

Under those conditions, the actual "green" you can play on is much smaller than it appears—so an unplayable area is a trap that will snare you, unless you know about it in advance. When you play a good wedge to a hole of that kind, and find yourself off the green, try to identify the *real* size of the green, and make your next goal simply to get the ball into that area and keep it there.

Even if you don't keep a precise map of every green you play, you may want to capture an image from Google Earth, trace the outline, and then shade off the portions that aren't playable, just to remind yourself that the green is smaller than it appears the next time you play the hole.

From off the green, prefer your putter if at all possible, because it is the club that gives the most precise distance control.

As long as the hole is at least 3 feet from the kind of hole that constitutes a "false green", the hole is playable. But you're going to need good distance control to make sure you get the ball into that area. (There is also an article at golf-info-guide.com that has a nice collection of tips on how to play a false front.)

On the other hand, if the hole is closer than 3 feet to a slope that won't allow the ball to stop, the green is basically unfair. Give it a try. But if you miss, and you aren't playing for serious cash, my best advice is to pick up your ball, give yourself a 3-putt, and move on (but don't count that hole in your putting stats!).

The Yips

The yips is the name for a condition in which you flinch as you putt. It's a condition in which you have no confidence in where the ball will go, and your very uncertainty causes you to miss, over and over, in a self-reinforcing feedback loop—what has been termed a "death spiral".

There are undoubtedly some cases that have a physical cause. The name given to the condition is "focal dystonia"—a situation where you have spasms in the small muscles of the hand. But if those spasms occur *only* when you're gripping a putter, something else may be going on.

How to Make Every Putt by Dr. Joseph Parent has a great bonus chapter, "One for the Yipper", that lists psychological causes and cures for this condition, where past flinching creates fear that causes future flinching. But as for the flinching itself, the cure may be as simple as training yourself to relax your hands!

Psychology or Physical Skill?

You'll notice this material on the yips is *not* in the next chapter on "The Mental Game", but here in "Special Situations". My personal belief is that while there are real psychological problems, people often attribute to "psychology" things they don't understand about physiology and mechanics.

In that sense, at least some problems that are regarded as "psychological" (such as "choking"), represent the "witchcraft" of the modern world. In the old days, anything people didn't understand—which was quite a lot—was attributed to the "gods". Then it was "witchcraft". These days, there is a lot we still don't understand, and when it comes to performance problems, a person's mental makeup gets the blame.

Don't get me wrong. Psychology and sports psychology are important disciplines that solve real problems. I just think that some problems that are said to be "in your head" can be addressed in better ways. If the solution to the problem is a *skill* that can be *learned* and *trained*, I believe that path represents a quicker and more certain solution.

In this chapter, I suggest that the problem is pretty much the result of gripping the club too tightly. It is possible to address deep psychological issues in an effort to learn to relax those muscles, but I suspect it is faster, easier, and more effective to *train* yourself to relax them.

I hope time will prove that assessment to be correct.

A Case of Forearm Tremors

While putting never presented a problem for me, I did have a very similar "flinching" problem for more than a decade. Any time I needed to move a spoonful of anything from one place to another, I had tremors in my wrist. My hand wound up shaking so hard that the spoonful went everywhere. To eat soup, I lifted the bowl to my mouth, so the spoon didn't have to travel so far. To put a spoonful of instant iced tea into a glass, I held the container very close to the glass.

The situation went on for a long time, and whenever I had a spoonful of anything, I worried. Was it the early onset of some severe neurological condition? Was I about to make a major mess and embarrass myself in public?

Because I worried, I gripped the spoon more tightly, attempting to keep it under control. Each time, the shakes appeared. Sometimes a little, sometimes a lot.

I wasn't having that problem anywhere else in my life, though. I could play musical instruments reasonably well and put a thread through a needle. So there did not seem to be any generalized neurological problem. Just a problem with the darn spoon.

After living with the problem for years, a thought occurred to me: What if I was gripping the spoon *too* tightly? Could it be the tight grip was *causing* the tremors?

It is no coincidence, I think, that I had that thought while working on this book. The next time I lifted a spoonful of instant iced tea from the container, I consciously relaxed my hand.

Guess what? No tremors.

Since then the tremors have come back only a couple of times— once when I was unconsciously gripping too tightly, and another time when my grip was *too* loose. In the first case, consciously relaxing the muscles did the trick. In the second, the solution was to focus on having a firm (still relaxed!) grip. Finding the balance was key.

I suspect that the yips are a manifestation of the same problem. Fear of missing the putt makes you grip the putter even more tightly, which *causes* the flinching that makes you miss. But the reality is that you only need to keep the putter from falling out of your hands, and that doesn't take much strength at all.

The key is to build up a "relaxation response" that kicks in the moment you take hold of your putter. Use any of the following ideas, singly or in combination:

- **Conscious Attention**
  As you hold the putter, focus your attention on the muscles in your hands and forearms, and consciously relax them. Do that every single time you hold a putter in your hands, until it becomes automatic.

- **Visualization**
  Think of your putter as a small baby bird. Cradle it gently, instead of squeezing the life out of it.

- **Yoga**
  Engage in a guided yoga practice where you consciously relax your entire body, one part at a time, starting from the toes and working to the head, or from the head to the toes. Start with a teacher or CD that takes you through the process, then learn to

practice it on your own while sitting or standing, as well as when lying down. After a while, you get very good at quickly scanning your body, feeling tense muscles, and immediately relaxing them.

- **A Hundred Straight Putts from *One Foot***
This one was recommended by my original instructor, Ed Tischler. Set up one foot from a practice hole that is on level ground, or one that is straight uphill from the ball. Putt a hundred balls, in sets of 3. After each set, empty the cup and putt the next 3 balls. If you miss one, start over. This exercise has multiple benefits—especially if you focus on relaxing your hands as you do it. (See the next section for more details.)

Fixing the Tremors

Playing a hundred straight putts from a foot away will begin to soothe your nerves, and create a repository of "success memories", which calms your brain with the certainty that yes, you are *perfectly capable* of putting down the line you intend. As you've learned, that is the first key to putting well!

Remember, the cup is only a foot away, so at the end of the follow-through, the face of the putter will be pointing directly at the cup (and be at least halfway there). It starts by facing the cup from behind the ball, and it ends facing the cup at the end of the stroke. That's all you have to do, every single time.

To make that process even more effective, focus on relaxing your hands, wrists, and forearms on each putt. That will be hard on your first few putts. But with the hole only a foot away, it will get easier and easier. By your hundredth putt, it will be second nature—and your confidence will have returned.

A hundred putts in a row *sounds* like a lot. But the hole is only a foot away, and you roll each new ball to the same position as the last one, so it doesn't take long. You just roll a new a ball into place, stroke, and get the next. The only thing that takes any time at all is taking the balls *out* of the hole. So use a practice hole that has a short flag with a saucer at the bottom, so you can lift the balls out easily. (Take them out after every three you've made.)

Also, it helps to have a hundred practice balls in a basket, lying on its side, so you can pull them out easily. Then, when you lift balls out of the hole, put them behind the hole. Seeing that pile growing larger and larger as you progress through the drill is a visual indication of progress that will inspire you and build confidence even faster.

By the time you have made a hundred in a row, your mental success repository will be well established—as will the habit of consciously relaxing your hands. The yips will also most likely be gone—because you will no longer be worried about your ability to putt down the line you're aiming on.

You may still miss putts, but with what you've learned in this book, you'll know that the miss was due to your speed or your read, and *not* your ability to putt straight.

Every Putt is a Straight Putt

Okay, you can do a hundred one-foot putts. What good is that?

A lot of good, actually. Remember: *Every putt is a straight putt to the target you've chosen*. If you can putt straight, and you can putt for a controlled distance, that's all you need to do!

**Every putt is a straight putt
to the target you've chosen.**

Here's the thing: When you're making a breaking putt, you just have to *start* the ball in the right direction. In effect, all you're doing is making a one-foot putt—but with a bit more force, so the ball reaches the hole.

If you can putt the ball straight for 12 inches, *you have all the skill you need* to putt down the line you intend. As Danny Willett was reported to have said while preparing to win the 2016 Masters, "Every putt is a straight putt for the first 12 inches". It's an old bromide, but still true.

**If you can putt straight for 12 inches,
you have all the skill you need.**

After that, it's all a matter of distance control, and choosing a good line. Because only on the most severely sloping and speedy green will the ball begin to break immediately after it leaves the putter. (And if it does, it's a pretty good indication that your line was too low.)

Doing 100 short putts in a row is worth doing at least once, if for no other reason than to prove you can. I did it early in my golfing career, because it was part of Ed's program. It seemed silly. Who can miss from 12 inches? But you know what? I lost focus a couple of times, and I *did* miss. After that, I learned to maintain mental focus until I sank a hundred of them.

That was a good learning experience in itself, but the real benefits kept coming. From that point on, there has never been *any* doubt in my mind that I can putt straight for 12 inches. Once you have done the drill, you *know* you have directional control. You can then focus your attention on the skill you *really* need—distance.

The Mental Game

To misquote Yogi Berra, putting is 90% mental, and the other half is between your ears. This chapter provides some useful techniques to help you relax and be confident in your play—including how to realistically rate your putts.

Learning to Relax

If you're playing a round of golf and missing putt after putt, without ever really knowing why, that's pretty stressful. When you step up to the next one, you have to wonder what you should do. Anxiety can easily take hold. However, when you begin consciously evaluating your putts, and know how to get accurate feedback, there is no mystery, and a lot less anxiety. So you rapidly begin to relax, without even being aware of it.

Too, you now know all you have to *do* is to identify the corrections you need to make. You can then relax, confident in the knowledge that the computer between your ears will take care of things.

Knowing *that* means you can play with confidence—because you know you are engaged in a *learning* process. You know you'll get better from green to green, and from round to round, for as long as you play the game!

If I could surgically implant one thought in your head, it would be this:

You are a great putter!
Time will prove it.

That, after all, is the premise of this book. *Everyone* can acquire the skill to be a great putter. It doesn't require enormous physical strength, or amazing reflexes, or any other rare attributes we associate with greatness. All it requires is a modicum of knowledge (which you now have), and your hard-wired, inalienable capacity to *learn*—something you couldn't turn off, even if you wanted to.

As you apply the techniques learned from this book, you should begin to notice improvements fairly quickly. You'll likely see putts coming closer than they have in the past, and you'll be automatically categorizing each missed putt (no matter who made it), knowing what went wrong in each case.

Recognizing those improvements and your increased understanding will help you relax, and it will help you build confidence—if not in your *present* ability, then in your *future* ability. Being more relaxed, and more confident, you will not only be a better putter, you will also have more fun in the process.

Breathing to Relax

If you *are* feeling a bit of stress, there are a couple of things you can do to relax. One is what the military calls the "combat breath". It's a simple *pranayama* (breathing) technique taken from yoga, but the military's idea of using it to slow down and relax in a stressful situation was nothing less than inspired.

To do it, breathe in for four seconds, and out for four seconds. (No need to use a watch. Just breathe in for a slow count of four, and breathe out to the same count.) That breath slows the heart rate, tamps down the adrenaline response, and helps you to be in the moment. Use it to combat stress—and to make your putting spectacular.

I use that technique on the "long drive" holes in my club tournaments. Coming up to a hole where everyone competes for the long drive of the day, I can be hurling drive after drive long and straight, right down the fairway. Then I come up to that hole, get a little tense, and try for extra distance. Result? An unplanned "cut shot"—in other words, a slice. Off the fairway, out of the competition. Drat! But my new secret weapon is that combat breath. "Works a charm", as they say in Ireland. (Also good for pressure putts!)

The other idea you can use is the double exhale, as described in The Putting Process chapter, under Step 5, Prepare to Putt, Double Exhale to Relax.

Confident Putting

The real beauty of knowing how to get feedback from your putts is that it *allows* you to keep your head down. You don't *have* to watch the ball as it travels to the hole. You can see where the ball ends up and know exactly what correction to make and how much correction is needed.

That's important because, as one professional teacher told me on the practice green, *the number one shot killer in the short game is lifting your head to see where the ball went.* (Some of the best advice I ever got.)

The number one killer in the short game is lifting your head to see where the ball went.

On a short putt, where you can see the cup out of the corner of your eye, you can stay quite still and listen for the sound of the ball dropping into the hole. If you don't hear anything, hold your position and tilt your head to see where the ball finished. On a longer putt, you can tilt your head after the ball leaves your field of vision, so you catch the last inch or two of the ball's travel, to confirm your read of the fall line.

With that information, you're going to get better with every ball you play. There is no need to raise your head, and everything to gain if you don't. So your confidence in your putting ability will translate directly into better putting.

No Pressure

You're faced with a putt of 15 or 20 feet. What are your odds of making that putt? Really. If you stood there for an hour and stroked a hundred balls, how many would drop? One? Two? Guess what? It's not that much different for professional golfers.

In his Putting Bible, Dave Pelz points out that even professionals have a 50% chance of missing from 6 feet away! And the odds of success drop rapidly from there.

Remember: The tiniest bump in the green can throw off the ball's distance or speed to make it miss—and there is more than one tiny bump on most greens. Depending on the quality of the green and the length of the putt, the ball may encounter quite a few of them. When a ball falls into the hole from far away, it's a wonderful thing, but it's not all that likely.

Also, remember that you're putting to a large target! Anywhere within 3 feet of the ideal target is going to leave a very makeable 2nd putt, and anything within 2 feet (a 4-foot target area) is a virtual gimme!

Then, too, if the ball just barely misses from, say, 15 feet away, the adjustment that would make it drop would have to have been a miniscule fraction of an inch. *No one* is capable of making that fine an adjustment. So if you get close, consider it a good putt. (I'll go into this in more detail in Rating Your Putts, next.)

Let's say that you're a short-distance putting wizard. (If you aren't already, you're well on your way to becoming one.) Any ball within 3 feet of the hole is virtually *guaranteed* to drop—*especially* if you were watching the ball as it came to rest, which gave you a good read on fall line and green speed. Now you're standing over that long putt. You know a 3-footer is virtually certain, and that holing out is virtually impossible. What is your goal *now*?

You're going to aim to get the ball to drop, of course. You're going to pick a target, judge the distance, and make your stroke to give yourself the best possible chance. But are you really trying to *make* that putt? Will you be upset if you miss? Hardly.

Given that a miss is all but inevitable, and that anything from 3 feet and in is a virtual certainty, all you really need to do on that long putt is to get close. And as you've already seen, to achieve that goal, all you really need to do is to be within the *vicinity* of the ideal target, as explained in You're Putting to a Large Target Area!

Rating Your Putts

Rating your putts helps take your mind off the score. Imagine, for example, you are 12 feet away and putt to within 6 inches. How good was that? It was *great*, wasn't it? Of course, it would have been wonderful if it dropped, but don't get mad because you missed the putt. Just take your feedback, rate the putt, and move on.

Oh yeah. And score the hole. But it's not about the score. The score is just a *reflection* of what you did. As long as you *learn*, you'll *improve*. And when *you* improve, your *reflection* improves. Don't be trying to score. That's like polishing a mirror to improve how you look. The score takes care of itself. Don't worry. All you really have to do is to keep learning from every putt you make, and be patient. Your looks will improve!

However, it is nice to know how well you did for any given putt. I use a rating system to give myself a grade. For anything longer than 10 feet, I use a scale like this:

- in the hole = PERFECT

- 6 inches or less = EXCELLENT (a tap-in!)

- within a foot (putter grip) = VERY GOOD or GREAT, depending on the original length

- within 2 feet (between grip and putter head) = VERY GOOD, should be an easy make

- within 3 feet (length of the putter) = OKAY

- within 5 feet = COULD BE BETTER (need more practice!)

- more than 5 feet = ARGH! (go straight to the practice green)

From 6–8 feet, I expect to be within a foot of the hole when I putt—but I won't be upset if the ball is 2 feet away, especially if the break was tricky. With the information I gained, it won't be hard to finish up.

The point is that not every putt has to be perfect. If you've left the ball in gimme range, that's as good as you really have to be.

Part V

//

Bonus Material

A COMPENDIUM OF additional information that covers

- A good sequence of activities for learning, practicing, and warming up.
- A detailed putting practice outline.
- The advantages of comparing to a *bogey* score, rather than par.
- Tips for saving your back.

Read the parts that interest you, or skip to the Epilog (page 215).

Learning, Practicing, and Warming Up

I believe strongly that golf skills are best learned by starting on the green and working back to the tee. I recommend that sequence for practice and warming-up, as well.

Other than playing, there are three types of skill sessions: learning, practicing, and warming up:

- When *learning*, a given session will be devoted mostly to working on one or two things.

- In a *practice* session, you'll spend time in one or more phases of the game—hopefully devoting most of your time to the phases in which you need more work.

- For a good *warm-up*, you'll do just a few things in each category to loosen up your muscles and get a feel for your swing, and then get on with the game.

How Much Practice Do You Need?

More practice is better (naturally), but how much is *enough*? The pros practice five or six hours a day—and they often *play* a round, on top of that. So they spend a full day working on their game.

(Interestingly, most professional musicians I know also spend five hours a day practicing. It's a matter of keeping their fine-motor skills in shape.)

Away from the pros, one low-handicapper I know has two practices a week, one for the short game and one at the range. *And* he plays every week. That's three times a week, every single week. Another plays *all* the time. And it works—each of them has a single-digit handicap.

The ideal, then, is three sessions a week—one for the short game, one at the range (plus some putting), and one to play.

The *absolute minimum* to maintain your skills is one session a week, cycling among those three.

However, a reasonably balanced approach that allows for significant improvement is two sessions a week, cycling through that set. A schedule like that should support a handicap somewhere in the teens.

So the first week, you have a short game session one day and the second session at the range. The next week, you play and have a short game session. The week after that, you go to the range, and then you play. And so on.

In each session then, you work in one of three areas:

- **Short game** (wedge play and putting)

- **Long game** (driving range, plus more putting)

- **Play** (course management, endurance, and target awareness—focusing on where you want the ball to go, rather than a lot of mechanical details)

For a single digit handicap, plan on three sessions a week. For a handicap in the teens, figure on two. To maintain a decent level of performance without being too serious about it, try to get out at least once a week.

If you have a lesson with a coach, that session takes the place of one of your practice sessions—and in your next practice session, you work on whichever phase of the game covers that lesson! Do that until you have ingrained what you learned, and *then* return to the cycling through the different phases of the game.

And, oh yeah, if you have extra time on your hands, you can work on the *trouble shots* such as greenside bunkers, fairway bunkers, and tough lies from under trees. The best way to do that is to make a note of the things you encounter when you play, then work on that area in a practice session. Or, if you really have lots of time, add a specific trouble shot session into your practice rotation.

Home Putting Drills

Practicing at home can make a huge difference in your scoring ability. It doesn't have to take very long, either. Just a few practice swings, several times a day, can help to ingrain things you're working on, and build "muscle memory" skills that pay off throughout your round.

For putting, you can do these:

- **Setup and alignment checks**.
  It only takes a moment to get into your setup position and check your alignment. Doing it often will pay huge dividends on the course.

- **Short putts to a target**.
  Try putting to a cup or glass, for example.

- **Longer putts** (up to 10 feet).
  For these, you'll need a putting mat. I like the SKLZ Accelerator Pro. It has a good surface, and a smooth ramp (which makes for an automatic ball return). Beware cheaper units. Some are just plain *terrible*, and definitely a false economy. (See Recommended Resources for details.)

A Standard Sequence of Activities

This section outlines a useful "standard" sequence for learning the game, for practicing, and for warming up to get ready for a round. (When learned in this sequence, each session can start with a review of what has gone before, and new skills can be "grafted" on to those that already exist.)

Putting Green

- **Short putts**
  Small swings, focused on direction control.
  Straight: uphill (1–2', 2–3', 4–5'), then downhill (2–3', 5–6')

- **Long "lag" putts**
  Longer swing, with focus on distance control.

- **Breaking putts**
  Medium and long distances on slow greens.
  Short distances on fast greens.
  Focus is on reading the green, choosing the line, and putting the right distance.
  – Perpendicular (cross line and fall line)
  – Diagonal putts (from the 45-degree angles)

- **Chips around the green**
  Basically just long putts with a bit of loft in the club. Focus is the same as on breaking putts.

Short-Game Area (or driving range, if necessary)

- **Longer chips**
  A somewhat longer swing with a focus on where the ball lands and how far it runs.

- **Pitches**
  Medium-to-full swing, with focus on hinging the wrists for loft and higher ball flight.

- **Flop shots**
  Open stance and open clubface, so the ball flies high and lands softly.

Tip:

Short-range chips and pitches are a great way to finish up the last few balls at the driving range. They don't take much effort, so they're a great way to cool down. Plus, you keep building skill in that critical area of the game. That strategy also lets you finish your long-club work after a good shot, so you can end on a high note.

Driving Range

- **Bump and run**

  Basically a chip shot using clubs with a longer shaft. Great for getting out from under trees to a known distance, and for keeping the ball flight low when there is a lot of wind. Also great to get the feel for each new club when you're learning, or any time your swing with a particular club has gone south.

  For practice and warm-up, make the longest chip you can with the 6- or 7-iron. (Thanks to PGA pro Bill Menkemeller for that suggestion.) Repeat with your longest hybrid, if you like, and you're ready for most anything that comes up during your round.

- **All clubs**

  I like to work with every other club on the way up, ending at the driver. Then I move to the 3-wood and do every club on the way down. When you are able to, work on shot *shape* (draw or fade):

  - Short irons
  - Long irons
  - Hybrids
  - Woods
  - Driver

Trouble Shots

- When learning, leave these shots for last, after you have a decent game from tee to green, *except* for trouble shots. Once you're at that point, add the trouble shots to your practice schedule, whenever you can fit them in:

  - Greenside bunkers
  - Fairway bunkers
  - Tight lies

- If you learn the game the way I did, you'll get *very* good at trouble shots from under a tree. That's because after teeing off, I was almost always playing from under one! In that situation, the low bump and run with a small swing is your friend!

For most of us, using the driver last is an ideal way to warm up for a round. That way, when we step up to the first tee, we're ready.

However, Jordan Spieth (world number one and Masters and US Open winner in 2015) started *and finished* his pre-game warm-up with his putter. If he has a late start time, due to his top-of-the-leaderboard position, he'll take a break after his first putting session and get some food. Then he goes to the range, working through the clubs in his bag, after which he goes to the short game area for lofted pitch shots and bunker shots. He finishes on the putting green, and *then* he's ready to play. He warms up his putting first and last. (If Jordan Spieth considers putting that important, who am I to argue?)

Practice Tips

Here are some general tips for your practices:

- A small, light practice bag that will hold a few clubs is ideal for a practice session. It's light, and easy to carry.

- When others are practicing, it's helpful to have balls that are distinctively colored or marked. Having balls in several colors is handy—or you can just use pink balls, like I do. (As far as I can tell, even the women don't use pink balls to practice!)

- When putting 10 balls, putting only 3 at a time keeps the path clear.

- A portable water bowl for small dogs is a great help. It sits open, will hold 10 balls easily, and can be folded up with the balls inside and kept in your practice bag.

- Successful shots go into the doggie bag. Those that weren't successful go back to the marker for another try. That way, when you've made all 10, you're ready to move on to another drill—and the dwindling pile of balls you're working with gives you a sense of progress. (And as the pile gets smaller, you have to walk more often to pick up your misses—that's your penalty!)

Putting Practice

The last chapter gave you general advice for learning, practicing, and warming up. This one gives you a detailed putting-practice checklist.

Check Your Setup

When you're first learning to putt, it's important to check these items every time. Later, it's important to "get a checkup" every so often, to be sure these mechanics are still in place.

1. **Eyes are over or just inside the ball.**

   Start by making sure your eyes are over the ball at setup, or close to it, so the line you're looking at when you're over the ball is the line you'll be putting on, using one of these techniques:

   ○ Use a plumb bob from the hardware store.

   ○ Hold an alignment rod by the tip, next to your temple.

   ○ Hold a ball at your temple and see where it drops.

   ○ Use a SKLZ Putting Mirror.

2. **You're aimed at your target.**

When you take aim at your target, make sure you're aimed where you think you are.

o Have someone place an alignment rod behind the putter, so it is pointing in the direction the putter is facing. Then step back to see where you were actually aimed. (Repeat until you're aimed where you think you are.)

o Have an alignment rod nearby, but not aimed at the target. When you're done setting up, move the alignment rod so it is touching each toe. Then step back. The rod should be parallel to the target line.

o Get one of the laser pointers that show where you're aiming, like the I-Putt laser. *After* you get set up, turn it on to see where you're aimed. Leave it on to get used to setting up with good alignment. Then turn it off and check again. Repeat until you are aiming where you *think* you are, 100% of the time!

Short, Straight Putts

With short, straight putts, the goal is to make sure the putter head stays square to the target line throughout the putt. If it does, the ball will go straight into the cup, with no argument—the first requirement for accurate putts.

Start by finding a straight putt no more than a foot from the hole, and putt 3 balls from there. If you make all three, you can move out to a longer distance. (Somewhere between 3 feet and 5 feet is plenty, for this drill. But you can play from even longer, just to test yourself and find out how straight your putts really are.)

If there is a slight slope, putt from directly below the hole, so you have a straight uphill slope. Any time you see a button hook at the end of the ball's travel, you're not quite below the hole. Move slightly to the side the button hook was on, until any ball that comes up short stops dead in its tracks, with no movement to the side.

Note:

If there is any doubt as to whether you are putting the ball straight or your read is off, there is a quick way to check. Use a couple of clubs side-by-side to make a ramp, or use the Green Speed Reader to roll the ball short of the hole. If it still button hooks, your read was off. If it goes straight, your putting stroke or alignment are off. (For help in that area, review the Putting Mechanics.)

If you're warming up for a round, 3 putts are plenty from any given distance. (I might putt 3 from a foot away, then 3 from 2 to 3 feet. If I'm feeling good, I may do 3 more from 5 feet or so.) The goal of warming-up is simply to get ready. So take feedback from each putt, and move on.

If you're practicing, and you're sure of your ability to putt it straight, 3 from any given distance is also plenty. Just get your putting warmed up, and move on to other drills.

If you're practicing and you're *not* sure of your ability—say, because you missed one of the 3 from close range—then putt 3 balls at a time until you make all 3 at least three times in a row (9 balls, in total).

If you're having trouble in this area, putt a tenth ball, and keep track of how many you made. If you made 7 putts from 3 feet, for example, your score is 70%. Your goal is 100% from 3 feet or less, and 80% or better from 5 feet. (Do not keep score when warming up for a round. A warm-up is a warm-up is a warm-up. Just get your muscles loose and relax.)

Another way to do the drill is to keep doing it from a given distance until you get 10. They don't have to be in a row. You just need to get 10. From 6 inches to a foot, you'll probably make 10 putts and be done. From 5 feet, maybe you have to make 50 putts to sink 10.

The nice thing about that strategy is that you automatically do more work where you need the most improvement. To track your progress, count your misses. The ideal, of course, is zero misses for 10 putts—first from one foot away, then from 2 feet, and so on, out to 5 feet. (But at the longer distances, you need a really smooth green.)

On the other hand, you don't really *need* to track progress. If you keep going until you've made 10, you'll have done all the work you need. Just be sure to keep that drill in the practice rotation, so you come around to it again.

Keep things moving along. Don't go to a longer distance until you make 80% from the distance you're at—the first time. You can do another set of 10 (or even two sets) if you want, but if you missed 80% in the first set, that's your longest distance for the day. (Even if it's only a couple of feet!)

Another way to do those drills is to putt another set from a shorter distance, if you're under 80%. (If you miss one from a foot away, you start at 6 inches!) In addition to acting as a "penalty" for missing, it ensures that you finish on a note of success.

That practice also tells your brain the distance from which you can *expect* to hole a putt—information you can use in two ways. For one, that distance defines the size of your ideal target area for longer putts. For another, it means that when you miss from farther out, you can relax! (Even though you would have *liked* to have made it, you didn't really *expect* to.)

Longer, "Lag" Putts

The goal with "lag" putts is to get a sense of green speed, and to develop the ability to putt to a given distance with a fair degree of accuracy. That is the second requirement for good putting.

To warm up and practice lag putts, you'll putt from a distance of 10 yards or more, but a successful putt is to *within an acceptable distance* of the hole, which, of course, depends on how far away you were at the start.

To make a measurement, put the putter head in the hole and bring it close to the edge. If the ball lies somewhere along the shaft, before the bottom of the grip, it is within 2 feet of the hole. That's the distance you want for an intermediate-length putt (say 10–15 feet). If the ball lies within the entire length of the putter, it is within 3 feet. That's plenty close for a longer putt (20–30 feet).

As you warm up and practice, focus on observing how far the ball travels at a given pace in the following drills:

- Putt 3 balls in a row. Wherever the first one goes, try to make the next two match it. (Ideally, one of the next two will tap the first one. The idea is to build a consistent, repeatable swing.)

- Putt a few balls to a distant spot on level ground. The idea is to build your ability to putt to a specific distance.

- Putt a few balls uphill to a distant spot.

- Putt a few balls downhill to a specific spot.

- If the green has grain, putt a few balls with the grain and a few against it.

- Put down a tee or marker 10 yards from a cup, and putt from the marker to the cup.

- Gradually move the marker farther away, 5 yards at at time.

For a warm-up, putt 3 balls and see how close you come. For practice, do 10 and track your percentage, or keep doing them until you get 10 within the acceptable range for your starting distance.

Be sure to tilt your head after putting, without lifting it, and hold your finish position until the ball comes to a stop, so your mind-body computer can correlate the size of your swing with the distance the ball travels.

Breaking Putts

Practice breaking putts to groove in your green-reading ability.

- Find the perfect "sidehill" putt, from a point on the cross line.

- Putt three in a row, using feedback from each putt.

- Keep adjusting your aiming point until the ball is consistently coming to a stop near your sight line (which tells you how much break you need to read for a given slope). Then work on your speed to get the ball into the hole.

- If you're warming up and you sink the third, even from a considerable distance, you're ready.

- If you're practicing, putt 10 and keep track of your percentage, or keep putting until you make 10.

- Repeat the drill from the other side of the hole, so you get used to looking at putts that break both ways.

- As always, watch the ball disappear from your field of vision, then tilt your head to see where the ball ended up, rather than lifting it, and hold your finish position until the ball stops moving. If you do those things, your mind-body computer will rapidly learn and improve.

With what you've learned in this book, breaking putts should start to become relatively easy. Even long breaking putts will become manageable, when your goal is simply to get them within 3 feet of the hole so you can sink them. And even if they wind up farther away than that (up to 5 feet), the information you will have gained about the green slope and speed will give you a good chance to drain the follow-up putt.

Goal-Oriented Putting Practice

This section ties together the material you've seen so far to create an efficient sequence for putting practice.

First, warm up with: short, straight putts; then medium-length, straight putts; and some long-distance putts to get a feel for green speed.

After warming up, the key is goal-oriented drills. They function like a game. You're keeping score, which keeps you engaged. And because you do each drill until you reach your goal, you automatically spend more time in the areas where you need the most work.

Goal-Oriented Drills

1. Short-range circle drill:

   ○ Make 3 from each of the eight main compass points (N, S, E, W, NE, NW, SE, SW).

   ○ Track the number of putts needed to make 3.

2. Lag putts:

   ○ Putt 10 to a target area.

   ○ Target area is anywhere between one foot from the hole to 4 feet from the hole, depending on distance from the hole and your skill level.

   ○ Use the putter to measure:

   ◆ The grip is about one foot.

   ◆ The bottom of the grip to the putter head is about 2 feet.

   ◆ The full length of the putter is about 3 feet.

3. Long-range circle drill:

   ○ Make one from each of the eight main compass points.

   ○ Track the number of putts needed.

To improve, it helps enormously to track the number of putts it takes to reach each goal. The ideal, of course, is "no misses". (Fat chance.) But you should at least see improvement from week to week.

Tracking your shots lets you see that improvement, and it also lets you see where you need work.

2-Putt Game with a Partner

Putt to a variety of holes, anywhere from 15 feet (5 paces) to 45 feet (15 paces) from the hole. So, on a practice green, you can play "18 holes".

If you're working on your stroke, pick a flat green or make straight uphill putts. If you're working on green-reading and putt-evaluation skills, then breaking putts are great.

If playing with a partner, each plays one ball. Winner chooses the next hole, and goes first. Keep score, and play for the first round of drinks or a dollar, but there should be something on the line to make each ball a small "pressure putt".

Solo 3-Ball, 2-Putt Game

For solo practice, play 3 balls. Make your lag putt with each of the three, then attempt to hole out the balls from wherever they finished. The goal is to 2-putt every shot. The penalty for a miss will be extra strokes from that spot.

Tip:

For the second putt, start from the ones that are closest in and work out to the ones that are farther away. Playing the shortest balls first clears the way for the longer ones. It also gives you another opportunity to read the green for the longer putts. (My thanks to Ed Tischler for that idea.)

After you've finished playing your original shots (and any penalty shots) to one hole, move to different hole, at a different distance, from a different angle.

For a mid-range practice, it would be great to hole the second putt every time. But I'll take two out of three, for a tricky read. For a long-range putt, I'd like to get two out of three, but one out of three is okay, too, if I do no worse than 3-putt on the other two. (Outside of 20 feet, 3-putts are going to be pretty common. Outside of 30 feet, they're pretty much a given.)

The Rules

- The goal is to 2-putt every ball, or better—but 3 putts are allowed for holes that are far away.

- Stroke your first putt for each of the 3 balls:

  ○ If it lands within 3 feet, superb.

  ○ If it is within 6 feet, it's okay.

  ○ If beyond 6 feet, it's a "muffed putt".

- Take your second putt with each of the balls in turn.

  ○ Start with any muffed putts that are on your way to the hole.

  ○ Leave the others for last.

- For each muffed putt:

  ○ Your goal is take no more than 2 additional putts with that ball.

  ○ If you leave the next putt close to the hole, it's good. If not, mark the spot.

  ○ If you don't hole out on your next stroke, you must 2-putt 3 balls from the original location, before going to a different hole.

- For the okay putts (within 6 feet):

  ○ Your goal is to hole out the putt.

  ○ If you don't, mark the spot.

  ○ Your new goal is to hole two out of three from that location, before going to a new hole.

- For good putts (within 3 feet):

  ○ Your goal is to hole out the putt.

  ○ If you don't, mark the spot and hole 3 out of 3 from that location, before moving on to a new hole.

Playing Against the Bogey Man

I am quite steadfast (fierce, actually) in my opinion that golf is a lot like playing a musical instrument. Both require fine-motor skills and synchronized timing. Both need to be practiced on a daily basis for the requisite skills to be learned and maintained.

Women's PGA golfer Cheyenne Woods (niece of Tiger Woods) put it succinctly in a recent advert for Volunteers of America: "I spend about two hours a day on my swing, another two on my short game. Every day. Because hard work is the only way to improve your game. That's just what you have to do".

That's a good indication of the amount of practice it takes to maintain the skills needed to play par-quality golf at the professional level. Of course, most of us are playing from shorter tees on easier courses. But it will still take a significant amount of daily practice to acquire and maintain par-quality golf skills. To even play at the bogey level requires a fair amount of practice—but it is an amount that is manageable for the average player.

To my mind, then, the concept of "par" is best reserved for professionals and those who have the time to practice every day. For the rest of us, "beating the bogey man" is a more reasonable goal.

Keep Score More Easily

When I'm using a scorecard, I take the first row after the one that shows par for each hole, label it with a "B", for bogey man, and fill in it in by adding one to each par score. That is the bogey row. So if the front nine and back nine each total 36, I know that the bogey total is 45, and the final total is 90.

Then, when I play, I score a plus or minus of that number for each hole. So +1 for a hole is one over bogey, and so on. In the row I use to keep my scores, I keep a running total of those pluses and minuses. So if I was +2 on the last hole, and −1 (par!) on the current hole, then my running total is +1.

When I'm playing against the "bogey man", an outing is eminently successful if my final score is less than a bogey score—and quite a lot of fun if is not too far over that.

Besides keeping me sane, that system makes it easy to keep score. The pros keep score as plus or minus compared to par. Fine for them. My way, I can do the same thing. Because I'm keeping a running total, I know at the end that if my running total is say, −4, and bogey was 90, then my final score was 86. Easy!

Take the Pressure Off Your Game

At the start of this book, I mentioned that the goal was to get on the green with one shot, *reliably*. And to 2-putt from there, *regularly*. Those goals fit quote nicely into the concept of playing bogey-level golf.

If you can 2-putt every green, then from anywhere near the green a decent short game shot should almost guarantee an *amateur up and down*—get the ball on the green within a reasonable range, lag the ball close, and tap in for a bogey.

With that kind of thinking, your goal from the tee is not necessarily to get on the green in regulation (although it's great when you do), but rather to get *within range* of the green, or *greenside* in regulation (see the "Amateur Stats" sidebar).

Once you're near the green, good wedge-play skills, coupled with your green reading and putting skills, are going to give you a great shot at a bogey score (and a reasonable chance for some pars).

Amateur Stats

You have probably heard of the pro stat "greens in regulation" (GIR). It tracks their performance from tee to green. If they are on the green with 2 strokes left to make par, they got to the green in the "regulation" number of strokes.

For the rest of us, I propose an amateur GIR (green, *in range*) or *Greenside* In Regulation. If I get the ball in the *vicinity* of the green in the regulation number of strokes, my play from tee to green has been rather good, thank you very much. (On a par 4, that's one long drive that finds the fairway, followed by another long, straight shot.)

I may not be on the green at that point, but I'm dead happy with my play so far, so I call it an amateur GIR. From there, I should be able to get on the green in one more stroke. If I can 2-putt from there, I have an amateur up and down. That stat is one stroke more than a pro's "up and down" stat, which is one stroke to get on, and another to get in, which saves par from off the green.

An amateur up and down, on the other hand, is one stroke to get *on* the green, another to get *up* near the hole, and one more to get *down*.

An amateur GIR plus an amateur up and down makes a bogey score! I'll get the occasional par and the rare birdie. And I'll take some double bogeys. But on a good day, it all averages out to bogey. And given that I don't practice every day, that's a darn good score.

Make the Bogey Man a Moving Target

As you improve, you can gradually reduce the size of the bogey man you're playing against.

On most scorecards, the holes have an additional, smaller number. That number reflects the hole's difficulty, relative to other holes on the course. So the #1 hole is the most difficult, the #2 hole is the second most difficult, and so on.

Let's say you've started to cut the bogey man down to size, and now you want to play against 2 under bogey, instead of bogey. On the scorecard, find the #17 and #18 holes, and write in par for those holes in the bogey row. For the remaining holes, add one to par for the bogey score. Since you've cut 2 strokes off the bogey score, the "bogey total" for the round is now 88, rather than 90. If you wound up at −1 for the round, then you shot 87.

There's nothing that says you have to use the same number on every course, either. On your municipal course at home, maybe you play against 16, or even 15. On a really difficult course, maybe you play against the full 18—or more. You can play against a higher number by adding one to several of the hardest holes, starting with the hole that is rated number one in difficulty.

In effect, you are giving each course a "rating", the same way the PGA does. The PGA calls it the *slope*, because it's a curve that describes how well a par golfer will play on that course, as compared to an average golfer. (On a tough course, a par golfer will avoid most of the trouble and will tend to play only a little worse than on an easier course. An average golfer will run into all of the trouble there is, and score *much* worse.) The PGA then uses your handicap (which is actually an *index*, these days) to look up your *course handicap* (the handicap you play against for a given course).

The PGA system works beautifully, but it's complex. And you need an official handicap to make it work. Most of us play on courses close to home. Using the "variable bogey" system, the bogey man becomes a moving target that can be adjusted for each course.

When to Play for Par

As you improve, you're going to find that some holes are well enough within your ability that you should be playing for par. I call those holes *reachable*.

I don't know about you, but my chances of getting on the green with a long iron or hybrid are pretty slim. It's great when it happens, but I don't count on it—so when it comes to betting, I'm keeping my money in my pocket.

With my wedges and (very) short irons, though, I can be pretty deadly. With my game, that works out to be about 130 yards away. So a short par 3 in that range is "reachable", in my world—and that is a hole I *should* be able to par.

Similarly, if the distance that remains after a reasonable drive on a par 4 (or a drive and a long shot on a par 5) is 130 yards or less, the hole is reachable. For those holes, it makes sense to play for par, rather than bogey.

Of course, determining which holes are reachable comes down to understanding how well you play! But once you have that understanding, you may find that on most courses, 9 out of 18 holes are reachable, even for an average player. (Once I started identifying reachable and unreachable holes, I found that *most* courses are divided pretty evenly between the two.)

For such a course, the "bogey" column becomes a "goal" column, labeled with "G". In that column , you write in par for the reachable holes, and bogey for everything else. If 9 of the holes are reachable, then instead of having to choose between playing for 72 (par) or 90 (bogey), your target is 81, reflecting the 9 reachable holes. You can then record your score as a plus or minus against your goal for each hole.

Interestingly, that level of play equates to a single-digit handicap! If par is 72, and bogey is 90 on a course where 9 holes are reachable, a goal score of 81 is exactly 9 more than par!

So while par-level golf is a pipe dream for most, and bogey is a decent goal for the average player, playing in the low 80's or high 70's is a good goal for someone who wants to achieve real proficiency. Identifying reachable holes and making par on them is a great way to achieve that goal.

Preventing Back Strain

(Originally published at TreeLight.com in *Putting Games.*)

The first time I started doing a lot of putting, I noticed that my back hurt. That turns out to be a pretty common complaint.

The trick is to push your butt out. That simple move makes you bend at the hips, instead of the waist. That's important, because when you bend at the waist, you're bending your back. It's a tip you can use when you work on your chipping, as well.

The difference is pretty amazing. When you bend at the hips and your back is flat, there is no strain at all on your back! In that position, the strain is on the muscles of your backside and your hamstrings. The only time there is strain on your back is when your back is bent.

I originally learned the ideal position for a proper "deadlift" from a book on kinesiology by Dr. Michael Yessis. That is the position you want.

To find that position, first push your butt out, so you're bending from the hips. Then arch your upper back slightly (*not* your lower back), so you're looking a little ahead, rather than down at the ground. Now, while you're bent over, tuck your butt all the way under. Then push it all the way out again. The position right in between those two extremes is the *flat back* position.

In that position, you'll find that your knees have automatically bent a little, and that your arms are hanging loosely, just in front of your knees. In other words, you are in the *perfect athletic position* you need for virtually every sport.

Perhaps most importantly, when you're lifting things, that positioning tells you when to use your legs. When you can't lean forward any further without bending your back, *that's* when you need to bend your legs. (The common advice to "use your legs" isn't very good, because it's entirely possible to bend your legs *and* bend your back at the same time, which is not helpful.)

Important:

I like to say that when you have the right technique, you can safely attempt to lift a piano—it may not move, but you won't kill yourself trying. However: Do NOT do that just because you read it here. Have someone who knows check your technique. Reading about it is one thing. Doing it right is another. Note, too, that is entirely possible to strain a muscle, even with the right technique. (I've done so. It heals.) The important thing is to prevent "throwing out your back" in the process.

The same technique used in the momentary effort of a weightlifting "deadlift" is equally applicable to the sustained effort of putting or chipping practice. Do your best imitation of a knuckle-dragging great ape, and you'll have the perfect position for your back.

Practicing that position can also help your golf swing! When your lower back is in the neutral position halfway between having it pushed all the way *out* and having it tucked all the way *under*, you can turn your body more freely, and do it without stressing your lower back. (My thanks to Pete Dooley, at GolfTec for alerting me to that fact.) For more on this important subject, read How to Use Biomechanics to Save Your Back and Your Golf Swing, by Richard Olshock.

Part VI

Epilog

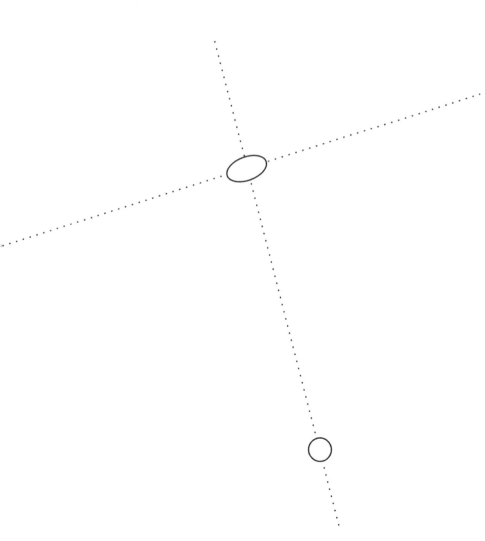

The Pioneer of Vector Analysis

After finishing this book, just before sending it to press, I stumbled across a reference to a book written in 1984. That book pioneered the use of vector science to the problem of putting.

I like to give credit where it is due. The author of that book was H.A. Templeton, and the book was called *Vector Putting: The Art and Science of Reading Greens*. (I'd also like to credit Geoff Mangum, whose online PDF, *Optimal Putting*, referenced that book.)

That book is long out of print, and doesn't appear to be available anywhere these days. But when I found a diagram from it on the web, it struck a chord.

Back around 1984, I was making my first forays into the world of golf. I wouldn't play regularly for another decade, and wouldn't take the game *seriously* for another five years after that. But as is my habit, I'm sure I perused the bookstores for information on my latest hobby. (I always do, so I'm certain I did!)

I never bought that particular book, but as I said, that diagram struck a chord. I have a strong suspicion that I *browsed* it, once upon a time.

I began writing this book from the standpoint of *feedback*, after watching the greatest players in the game laboring under inconsistent conditions. As I began looking for a way to evaluate putt results into their speed- and read-components, I suspect that the idea of vector analysis bubbled up from my subconscious.

So Templeton may well have given me the idea for how to explain green reading and putt evaluation—in which case, we owe him a debt of gratitude!

What's Next?

I f you've worked through the book to this point, then congratulations! You've acquired a lot of information that will be of practical use every time you play.

It may have taken a bit of work to put the picture together. But now that you have, the reward for your effort is a lifetime of understanding—and the steady improvement in putting skill that will result from your newfound knowledge.

You've learned how to read a green, and how to predict the ball's movement as it encounters different slopes on the way to the hole. You've learned how to *evaluate* the results of a putt, to get the all-important feedback you need to refine your read and speed. Most importantly, thinking in terms of *vectors* has begun to become a habit—because that is the major key that unlocks *all* of the green's secrets.

After reading this book, the greens will have begun to make sense. *Because* they make sense, you'll better understand your misses. With that understanding, you'll improve rapidly.

That has been my experience, at least. Putting now makes perfect sense to me and has become a very enjoyable part of the game. Over a round, I typically have more 1-putts than 3-putts, so I average a little less than 2 putts per hole.

To paraphrase an old martial arts saying, before I started this investigation, "A green was just a green. A putt was just a putt." Things were simple. But they were also *mysterious*. I didn't really understand how things worked.

As I dove in, "A green was no longer a green. A putt was no longer a putt." In other words, things became more complex. You may well have had that experience while reading this book.

But once I understood the basic principles and internalized them then, once again, "A green was just a green, and a putt was just a putt." That is where you're headed.

Yes, the greens became simple, once again. But now, I had true understanding. And I had *confidence*. It felt as if there was no green in the world I couldn't 2-putt.

Of course, it requires practice to develop the requisite skill, but now I knew *exactly* what went wrong, on every putt I missed. And I improved my read with every putt I watched—regardless of whether or not it was on the same line as mine.

These days, putting is a *given*. I have now switched focus to my swing and my short game. The goal is to get closer to the hole with the short game, to up my 1-putt percentage, and to improve my swing so I'm in *position* to go low more often.

If you recall, the investigation that led to this book began when I got sick and tired of throwing away a good score after getting oh-so-close to the green. Instead of taking 3 shots to get on the green, I wanted to get on in one. *Reliably*. And instead of taking 3 putts to get down, I wanted to get down in 2. *Regularly*.

To do that, I needed a good short game, and good putting skills. I set about investigating how to understand and acquire those skills. The results of my findings on putting constitute *Comprehensive Keys to the Green*. Then what about the short game?

To me, the "short game" is any distance shorter than a full swing from the fairway with your smallest club. For most of us, that's about 60 yards. So anything less than 60 yards constitutes the short game.

I began looking for *invariants* in the short game—things you could hang your hat on, things that did not change depending on the weather or the phase of the moon.

I'm happy to say that I've identified several such invariants that I now use to get on the green in one stroke from virtually anywhere within the short game range. I look forward to sharing those tips with you in the next volume.

The next volume?

Yes. My original intent was to cover the skills needed for both putting and the short game—what Dave Pelz calls "the scoring game"—in this volume. But length considerations and the need to find answers for several critical questions made it necessary to create two books instead.

However, I can say that the two skills (putting and the short game) are inextricably woven together. In the long game, the problem is mostly *direction control*. You can be a little long or a little short, but you really don't want to be off line. And of course, you need a decent swing.

But in the short game and in putting, the problem is mostly *distance control*. Because the distances are small, *everyone* has the capacity to master the swings needed to achieve those distances. But you need to know how. And that is the information I want to share.

Putting and the short game have other things in common, as well: Your ability to read a green and predict break helps you select a *target* for your short game shot; and the results you get from that shot help you refine your read and speed when it's time to putt.

As I mentioned, these days I consistently get on the green in one stroke. But I want to improve enough to get close to the hole, to up my percentage of 1-putts. And I plan to continue honing my putting skill, so I drop more medium-length putts in the 5- to 8-foot range.

Taken together, improvements in my short game (the next book), and continued refinements in my putting (this one) will increase my "up and down" percentage—as they will yours. In other words, if I'm anywhere *near* the green in regulation, par is in sight.

That just leaves the full swing. That's a requirement, in order to get somewhere near the green "in regulation" (that is, with 2 putts left to make par). After nearly a hundred hours of lessons, and many more in practice, I'm *beginning* to get a solid grasp of that subject.

To re-tool the swing, I have been doing a lot of "homework"—in the form of slow-motion drills I can do at home—to retrain my brain to perform a more effective, more reliable swing. I look forward to sharing those drills, and the science behind them, in a future book on the full swing.

After all, we can create a black belt martial artist in a couple of years. In that time, you can acquire enough skill to save your life. But when it comes to golf, people spend *years* trying to find something that works. Most never do. They continue to struggle.

My take is this: If lives depended on having a good golf swing, we would find better and more effective ways to teach it. A person shouldn't have to search for a swing for more than a decade, as I have done. It should be possible to develop a solid swing in the same time it takes to develop a black belt—two years, *at most*. And a decent level of proficiency should be achievable in half that time.

Of course, with as many as 19 moving parts that have to be timed just right, the golf swing is by far the most complicated movement in sports. Mastering it is a lot like mastering the violin. It takes time.

But building up that skill should be a matter of figuring out the right sequence of activities. Done right, each new activity should add one more element to the movement pattern, until a reliable full swing emerges.

That's what I'm working on now (in addition to the short game). Because being *in position* to go low means being near the green in regulation. And getting to that position requires a good swing.

So there you have it:

1. A good swing puts you in position (on or near the green) in regulation.

2. A good short game puts you near the hole, for an up and down.

3. A good putting stroke puts you in the hole from short-to-medium-range, or near it from long range.

With those skills in place, golf remains challenging, but it's a lot more fun. As for learning those skills, I maintain they are best learned starting from the green, and working back to the tee.

This book gives you the keys to master the greens. You might even consider it a master's degree in green reading. The next volume will give you the keys to the short game. As I continue working with my coaches, and continue experimenting, the plan (or maybe hope) is to develop a great swing—and to figure out a good way to teach it.

As always, I'm a big fan of anything that works. I'll be investigating anything that looks promising, and passing on the credit whenever I can. For example, I plan to investigate the Tabata system of instruction, which is based on martial arts principles. As a former martial artist and martial arts instructor, I can appreciate that approach. I look forward to sharing what I learn.

There are many golfers and touring professionals who have acquired a great swing—but they are still a very small percentage of the golfing population. I think most of them stumbled across a decent sequence of activities, generally with the help of one or more coaches. They then drilled until the skill became second nature.

I *expect* the process to take time and effort. But I *also* expect a well-defined progression for acquiring that skill. We have them in other sports—for example, in volleyball (which I used to coach). We should have a similar progression in golf. Once we do, I expect we'll see a decent surge in average skill levels.

That, as Don Quixote would say, is the quest. It's what I'm working on now. When it happens, I want you to be the first to know. To make sure, subscribe at my site, TreeLight.com, or follow me on Twitter: @ericTreeLight.

In the end, the best place to stand is on the shoulders of giants, where you have the best view. My role is to show you which giants give you the best vantage point, and how to find them.

Here's to playing the best golf of your life!

Glossary

above the hole – a position up the fall line from the hole (that is, above the cross line).

across from the hole – a position on the cross line.

below the hole – a position down the fall line from the hole (that is, below the cross line).

break – the distance the ball moves downhill due to the influence of gravity, when the ball is aimed at the ideal target. If a ball aimed 6 inches above the hole finishes inside it, then the putt on that green, from that distance, is said to have 6 inches of break.

cross line – a line through the hole that is perpendicular to the fall line.

downhill – the direction going down the fall line.

fall line – a line going through the hole, straight downhill (aka the gravity axis).

ideal target – the perfect target for the hole, such that a putt directed towards it, with the right amount of force, invariably drops in.

near target – a point slightly ahead of the ball, on the target line, that you use to help align your stance when you're setting up to putt. Watching the ball rolling over that point is a good way to ensure that the ball starts out in the intended direction.

read line – the sight line. If a putt ends on this line, you had the right read.

short game – This term is used in two distinct ways in the golfing world. Each meaning serves an important purpose, and neither has a good alternative, so the two meanings persist:

a. **wedge play *and* putting**
This is what most of us amateurs think of as "the short game". It's anything other than the full swings you take to get from the tee to (near) the green. The advantage of this meaning is that it lets you say things like, "to score well, you need a great short game". In that context, "the short game" obviously includes putting.

b. **wedge play only**
This is what most professionals think of as "the short game". In their statistics, they have separate categories for putting and the short game.

sidehill – the direction going across the hole, perpendicular to the fall line along the cross line.

sight line – a line going from the ball to the hole.

speed line – the fall line, or gravity axis. If a putt ends on this line, you had the right speed for the line you chose.

target line – the line from the ball to your *target* (your point of aim on the fall line).

"the line" – this is the common way of saying target line, the line from the ball to the ideal target. Reading greens is all about determining break, finding the right line. Making putts is about putting along that line with the right speed.

uphill – the direction going up the fall line.

Recommended Resources

As with all web-based resources, URLs and links can (and do) change. Every effort has been made to ensure these links are live and correct. But some of them may no longer work by the time this book reaches you.

Websites

http://keys2golf.com

Visit the website for additional articles and announcements, follow the blog, contact the author, sign up for announcements, and share information with other golfers.

http://www.puttingzone.com

Lots of good tips at this site, plus a downloadable PDF that is difficult to read, but which contains quite a few "golden nuggets" of information—several of which have found their way into this book.

Articles

http://www.treelight.com/golf/PuttingGames.html

A collection of putting games I learned from Ed Tischler, Keith Shepperson, and Jim Holmlund. Includes my notes on preventing back strain.

http://www.drputt.com/deardrputt/plumbob.php
Using the putter to plumb-bob a green.

http://espn.go.com/golf/news/story?id=1773250
All I Know by Jack Nicklaus. A concise summary of Jack's philosophies for playing the game.

http://www.golfdigest.com/story/10_rules_jim_mackay
10 Rules for Reading Greens
A nice collection of tips from Phil Mickelson's caddy, Jim Mackay.

https://www.youtube.com/watch?v=7vDwYzPGQ54
Reading Grain On Bermuda Greens.
Video that shows sample holes, and identifies the grain.

http://www.slideshare.net/BenchCraft/golf-tips-the-easy-guide-to-reading-the-grain-of-a-green
Golf tips: The easy guide to reading the grain of a green. A really nice slide show that shows how grain influences the ball's movement.

Apps and Devices

Green Speed Reader
A portable little device that unfolds into a ramp you can use to roll the ball in a consistent direction, with consistent force. It is basically a Stimpmeter (the thing the pros use to measure green speeds), but it is smaller and more portable. The designers cleverly made it exactly 2 feet long, and marked the edges so it doubles as a ruler you can use to make measurements, if you need to.

EyeLine Golf Sweet Roll Rail System
A large, semi-portable ramp and putting trainer. At $100, this ramp is the Cadillac of ball-rollers. If you want to do a large, full size experiment, this device is the way to go.

BreakMaster Digital Green Reader
At $120, it's pretty expensive, but it has the advantage of telling you how *much* the green slopes, as well the direction it is sloping in. It's a great practice tool to improve your green-reading accuracy, if your budget allows it. It says that the arrows point to the eight cardinal compass directions (N, NE, E, etc.), but when the slope direction is between any two of them, both arrows are shown. In effect, then, it points to one of 16 directions—close enough, for most of us.

Momentus EEZ-READ Green Reader
A much less expensive bubble level, at $25. Gives a very accurate indication of break direction, but not of the amount of slope. (The distance from the center gives you an idea, but it's hard to tell if you're on a 2-degree slope or a 4-degree slope, for example.)

Note:
There are cell phone *apps* that do a similar job for a dollar, but the ones I found came up short in the usability department. The BreakMaster app (unrelated to the digital device) had a non-stop revolving arrow, and the support address no longer works, so it was impossible to ask them to turn it off. The Break Reader app was free, but the ads were a major annoyance. You might want to see what's available, though, before spending your hard-earned cash. Somewhere, sometime, *someone* will probably get it right.

Books on Putting

Dave Pelz's Putting Bible
Detailed, comprehensive analysis. I believe that the vector analysis I have provided in this book makes a great addition to the information he has provided.

How to Make Every Putt by Dr. Joseph Parent
Sound advice on putting and the mental game.

How to Use Biomechancs to Save Your Back and Your Golf Swing by Richard Olshock.
Terrific little volume that tells you both *why* and *how* to get to a neutral back position. Includes a video on the little-known *peroneus* muscle at the side of your rear leg, and the role it can play both in protecting your back and improving your swing.

Optimal Putting by Geoff Mangum (PDF)
A difficult read that nevertheless contains some golden nuggets of wisdom. It's a free download, so it's worth skimming past the detailed science to get to the tips you can use. (In addition, it references the *Vector Putting* book!)

Putt to Win by Dave Stockton
Great book on putting technique.

SPeeD Practice Drills by Roy Day
A great collection of drills you can use to improve your putting. Currently out of print, but worth getting secondhand if you can find it. He has other books that give drills for the driving range, chipping, and pitching, as well.

Vector Putting: The Art and Science of Reading Greens by H.A. Templeton (1984).
Long out of print and no longer available, this book (summarized here) introduced the idea of using vectors to understand how putts work. Unfortunately, it made the mistake of trying to accurately predict the amount of break to expect—something that is theoretically possible, but difficult to do reliably (or quickly!) in practice. Still, the concepts in that book predate this one, which stresses the importance of deriving accurate feedback. The other drawback to that book, according to one reviewer, is that it only works on a flat surface with a consistent slope, which is addressed in this book by the feedback concept and in the chapter on Reading Contours.

Training Aids

The links here are to known products of good quality on Amazon. By all means, find a local store where you can try them and, if possible, compare them to similar products. There may be others that are better, or possibly cheaper. If so, please drop me a note at keys2golf.com.

SKLZ Putting Mirror

> Great way to check your alignment when you address the ball with your putter.

I-Putt laser

> Handy little device that clips onto your putter shaft, so you can see where you're actually aiming. Invaluable to check your alignment, as described in Check Your Setup.

SKLZ Accelerator Pro Indoor Putting Green

> One of many devices on the market that will help you to groove in a straight putt. It has a firm, consistent surface that putts true. Unfortunately, it also has a ramp at the end. That is a nice design that allows gravity to return the ball, and it helps to develop a firm stroke. When I started playing golf, those were both a big plus. But once I realized that dying at the hole is the ideal way to make breaking putts, it became clear that a flat version would be more useful, as it would help me to develop accurate distance control, as well as direction control. For direction control, though, the device is superb. It has lines that help to guide the putting stroke, and firm, consistent surface to roll the ball on.

> Beware of imitations! I once brought a competing brand from a reputable store, and it was so terrible I had to take it back (something I rarely do). The felt was soft, rather than firm, it came folded up rather than rolled, so there were creases that would never be flat, and the plastic ramp created a bump under the felt, which made the ball hop when it got there. Worse still, the felt dipped after the bump, creating a soft recess—a "tray" that trapped any softly-putted ball. In short, it was worthless, which motivated me to add a link to this book, in order to spare you a similar experience.

Instruction

AimPoint golf putting instruction
  http://www.aimpointgolf.com/
  A detailed program for identifying the amount of break needed
  for a putt, as a combination of slope, green speed, and distance
  from the hole. A bit complicated, but a real eye-opener when it
  comes to finding out how much break you *really* need to allow on
  a fast and/or steep green.

Bill Menkemeller, at the Pruneridge Golf Club
  https://vimeo.com/135102653
  If you're getting started and you live near Cupertino, California,
  you could do worse than take lessons from Bill. I started with him
  to get my full swing back in shape, so I could take advantage of
  what I had figured out about the short game. But right away, he
  had a huge impact on my chipping and pitching technique.

Ed Tischler's New Horizons Golf program
  http://newhorizonsgolf.com/
  Excellent instruction on the swing and the short game. An excep-
  tionally talented player and teacher who got me started on the
  road to playing real golf (at least until life intervened).

Dave Pelz short game schools
  http://www.pelzgolf.com/
  I have yet to take one of these myself, but there is no doubt in my
  mind that if you have anything like a decent swing, and you want
  to score low numbers, this is the place to go. (Or find a teaching
  pro near you who gives a short game clinic.)

Gary Pearce, at the Moffet Field Golf Club
  Gary was kind enough to give me a bunker-play lesson at Moffet.
  In the process, he demonstrated the skills of an exemplary PGA
  professional, as good at teaching as at playing.

GolfTec

http://www.golftec.com/

Superb instructional system where they put you in a belt and shoulder harness that tracks your body movements. They combine that data with video analysis, video comparison with similar-style tour players, and shot tracking. Also, an expert coach does the analysis and gives you drills you can do to make corrections.

Highly recommended. My coach was Pete Dooley, but everyone there seems to be quite good. His were the third set of lessons I took (After Ed and Bill.) The first session was an evaluation and half of a coaching session—in that single half-session he found the two glaring issues that were causing my slice and chicken wing (open shoulders at setup and bad club position at the start of the downswing). Those issues that escaped *everyone's* attention, until then. Needless to say, I'm a huge fan.

Pebble Beach Golf Academy

http://pebblebeach.com/golf-instruction-and-services/pebble-beach-golf-academy

Prestigious instruction facility, headed by PGA Teacher of the Year Laird Small. (Expensive, but worth every penny.)

About the Author

E RIC ARMSTRONG is an accomplished athlete and an amateur golfer. Using his analytical and investigative skills he, like all golfers, is continually working to bring his handicap down. In the past, he has worked in software development, technical writing, and marketing. Currently, he runs the TreeLight.com website, which he started in 1997. He lives in California, and is available for putting clinics.

Contact Eric and follow his blog through the website for this book:
keys2golf.com

Check out his health-and-fitness website:
TreeLight.com

Follow him on Twitter:
@ericTreeLight

About TreeLight

TreeLight.com was founded by Eric Armstrong in 1997 as a free-information site devoted to all aspects of health: fitness, nutrition, spiritual, social, and societal. Independently owned and operated, it takes no advertising and exists solely to provide useful information to the public at large. (It also provides links to recommended products at Amazon.com, which produce a modicum of income, as is the case with the eBook edition of this book.)

TreeLight PenWorks is an extension of the website that was formed to provide books like this one, to provide deeper, in-depth treatment of selected topics.

For other titles in the *Comprehensive Keys* series, visit TreeLight.com/books.

To subscribe for announcements of new books and articles, go to TreeLight.com/subscribe.html.